The Rule of Benedict

T0154148

Other Books in the
SkyLight Illuminations Series

The Rule of Benedict

Christian Monastic Wisdom for Daily Living— Selections Annotated & Explained

Annotation by The Rev. Dr. Jane Tomaine

Translation edited and adapted by
Sister Marilyn Schauble, OSB,
and Sister Barbara Wojciak, OSB

Walking Together, Finding the Way®

SKYLIGHT PATHS®
PUBLISHING
Nashville, Tennessee

SkyLight Paths Publishing
an imprint of Turner Publishing Company
Nashville, Tennessee
New York, New York
www.skylightpaths.com
www.turnerpublishing.com

The Rule of Benedict:
Christian Monastic Wisdom for Daily Living—Selections Annotated & Explained

Annotations © 2016 by Jane Tomaine
Translation © 1989 by the Benedictine Sisters of Erie

Library of Congress Cataloging-in-Publication Data
Names: Benedict, Saint, Abbot of Monte Cassino, author. | Tomaine, Jane, annotator.
Title: The rule of Benedict : Christian monastic wisdom for daily living : selections annotated and explained / annotation by The Rev. Dr. Jane Tomaine ; translation edited and adapted by Sister Marilyn Schauble, OSB, and Barbara Wojciak.
Description: Nashville : Turner Publishing Company, 2017. | Series: Skylight illuminations series | Includes bibliographical references and index.
Identifiers: LCCN 2016052608 | ISBN 9781594736322 (pbk. : alk. paper)
Subjects: LCSH: Benedict, Saint, Abbot of Monte Cassino. Regula. | Benedictines--Rules. | Monasticism and religious orders--Rules. | Christian life--Catholic authors.
Classification: LCC BX3004 .E6 2017 | DDC 255/.106--dc23
LC record available at https://lccn.loc.gov/2016052608

10 9 8 7 6 5 4 3 2 1

Manufactured in the United States of America

Cover Design: Walter C. Bumford, III, Stockton, Massachusetts; adapted by Thor Goodrich
Cover Art: Icon of St. Benedict written by +Sister Mary Charles McGough, OSB, © St. Scholastica Monastery, Duluth, MN. Used with permission.

To my husband, John,
for his love and presence in my life

Contents ■

Acknowledgments ☐

In the Rule of Benedict, chapter 3, "Summoning the Members for Counsel," Benedict quotes the book of Sirach to offer critical advice to monastic leaders: "Do everything with counsel and you will not be sorry afterwards" (Sirach 32:24 in RB 3.13). Writing a book is no different. I am indebted to the Reverend Canon C. K. Robertson, PhD, Canon to the Presiding Bishop of the Episcopal Church for Ministry Beyond the Episcopal Church, for his suggestion, intervention, and encouragement for this project. I am deeply grateful to SkyLight Paths Publishing for the opportunity to write this book on my favorite subject, the Rule of Benedict. I thank my editor at SkyLight Paths, Emily Wichland, for her graciousness, attention to detail, responsiveness, and editorial skill that made working together both pleasant and profitable. I also thank Jon O'Neal, managing editor at Turner Publishing, for his able help in seeing this book to completion. My gratitude flows out to two Benedictine monasteries who contributed to this project: Sr. Susan Doubet and the Benedictine Sisters of Erie for use of the inclusive language version of the Rule; and Sr. Beverly Raway, prioress, and the sisters of St. Scholastica Monastery in Duluth, Minnesota, for the use of the beautiful icon of Saint Benedict. I owe a debt of gratitude to three monastic scholars whose commentaries deepened my knowledge of the Rule: Terrence Kardong, Aquinata Böckmann, and Timothy Fry. Many thanks also to Benedictines who contributed helpful information about monastic life today: Sr. Laureen Virnig, oblate director, and Sr. Michaela Hedican, prioress, from Saint Benedict's Monastery in St. Joseph, Minnesota; Fr. Augustine Curley from Newark Abbey in Newark, New Jersey; Sr. Karen Joseph from the Sisters of St. Benedict in Ferdinand, Indiana; and Sr. Mary Forman from the Monastery of St. Gertrude in Cottonwood, Idaho. I appreciate the time taken by two friends, Benedictine oblate Rev. Laura Howell and Nancy Little, who read the manuscript and offered suggestions. I thank my dear friend of over forty years, Mary Beth Starrett, who read draft after draft and supported me with her cheering. There are not enough words to thank my dear husband, John, who once again provided patience, understanding, and love along with many dinners. Finally, to dear Benedict, my mentor and guide, bless you and thank you!

Introduction ▢

"I don't like rules."

My eyebrows lifted slightly. At the Episcopal church where I served as the priest, we had just begun a seven-week education and worship season focusing on the Rule of Benedict. My heart's desire was that *everyone* would see the value of Benedict's ideas.

I paused, hoping that the speaker of these words had not noticed my reaction. "Ah ... oh, I see." I then explained that even though written in the sixth century for monks in a monastery, the Rule of Benedict has so much to offer us. Benedict gives us ways to nurture respectful relationships, compassionate leadership, meaningful worship, and faithful prayer. He guides us in forming a heart open to God and others. He shows us practical ways to follow Jesus and bring his gospel alive in our lives and hearts.

"Many people today like us, who live outside the monastery," I continued enthusiastically, "have turned to the Rule as a guide for a God-centered life." I then paused, eagerly awaiting a positive response to my sales pitch for the Rule.

"Well," the disgruntled church member responded, "I still don't like rules."

You are holding a book with selections from the Rule of Benedict in your hands. Do you like rules? Even if you do not, or are unsure about rules, you might be simply curious to know what *this* particular Rule is all about. Maybe you recently visited a Benedictine monastery of women or men and want to know what guides their lives. You may be studying different forms of religion and this book is required reading. Perhaps someone mentioned finding the Rule of Benedict helpful and you are interested to learn what this ancient document might offer you. Or you may be exploring different spiritual texts to find guidance for your life.

Whatever brought you to this book, I welcome you and give thanks that you are here. I pray that these pages will inspire you to learn more about the Rule and Benedictine spirituality.

Why Explore and Follow This Rule?

When I was young, my mother planted morning glories alongside our screened-in porch. The flowers were a vivid blue and truly glorious. The plants flourished not only because the sunlight was perfect for morning glories but also because they had a trellis to guide and support them as they grew. Without that trellis the plants would have become untidy clumps that did not show the beauty of both flower and leaf.

Like the morning glories hooked to the porch trellis, the Rule of Benedict is a spiritual trellis that you and I can cling to that will guide our growth as people of God, helping to bring out the beauty within each of us. The Benedictine trellis can support our relationship with God and others, and can shape how our spirit unfolds through good works, prayer, worship, and a balanced way of living. The Benedictine trellis connects deeply to God, and so can foster a meaningful and fulfilling life.

People from all walks of life and all branches of Christianity have written about the influence of the Rule on their lives. Esther de Waal, noted Benedictine author and Anglican laywoman, follows Benedict "to discover how to be human now today, tomorrow and for the rest of my life."[1] "St. Benedict's concern," she explains, "is always to form the underlying attitude and motivation, 'the disposition of the heart', which determines the way in which we see and handle our lives."[2] This Benedictine heart reaches one hand to God and the other to the world. Visionary spiritual leader and Benedictine author Sr. Joan Chittister describes the Rule as "a model of spiritual development for the average person who intends to live life beyond the superficial or the uncaring."³ Even Buddhists have written about the value of the Rule, noting similarities between their spiritual practices and that of the Benedictine monastics.

Before we look at the Rule I would like to give you some background on early Christian monasticism to help you understand the tradition that formed the Rule. The chart that appears below presents the key figures in the development of this tradition with estimated dates drawn from a variety of sources. We will also look at the life of Benedict, his creation of the Rule, and its structure. We will close with a brief look at Christian monasticism and the use of the Rule today.

The Development of Christian Monasticism
Antony   251–356 CE
The Desert Fathers and Mothers   3rd–5th centuries
Pachomius   290–348 CE
Basil of Caesarea   330–379 CE
Augustine of Hippo   354–430 CE
John Cassian   360–435 CE
The Rule of the Master   early 6th century
Benedict   480–547 CE

The Roots of the Rule of Benedict: Early Christian Followers

For many years it was thought that Benedict's Rule was an original document created by Benedict. Scholarship now shows that he *did* create original sections but also drew from the monastic tradition and from earlier writings either verbatim or by incorporating ideas presented in these writings. To use modern terminology, he did not reinvent the wheel but included established practices from the tradition, shaping these and adding new practices to create the ideal he was seeking for his monastery.

The Rule of Benedict has its earliest roots in the deserts of Egypt. In the harsh environment of heat, wind, and sand, monastic spiritual practices took shape that centered around denial of self for God.

The Quest for God in the Desert

In the early centuries of Christianity there were times and places where being Christian was dangerous, even against the law. But many Christians accepted death rather than deny their faith. Being a martyr was seen as the most self-giving way to follow the example of Jesus, who gave his life by dying on the cross. The persecutions ceased in the early fourth century when Roman emperor Constantine accepted Christianity. Christians then sought another way to model the sacrifice of Jesus and dedicate their lives totally to God. Even before the persecutions had ended, zealous Christians were already creating this model. In the desert regions of Egypt and the Middle East, men and women from all walks of life left family and friends to live in solitude in the desert close to their villages and towns. They were not seeking mystical experiences but a life formed by Holy Scripture and dedicated to God, unceasing prayer, and fasting.

There is no biblical blueprint for the form of monasticism that grew from these early ardent and, some would say, extreme followers of Jesus. These early Christian women and men were influenced by Greek classical philosophers in both pattern of living and withdrawal from society.[4] In fact, the word "monk" comes from the Greek *monachos*, meaning "one who lives alone."

The Rule of Benedict rests on the shoulders of these early monastic men and women. We will see how they and subsequent generations in turn influenced the development of Christian monasticism by providing important traditions and practices that Benedict included in his Rule.

Antony: Father of Christian Monasticism

The monastic tradition that Benedict inherited was first shaped by Antony (251–356 CE), a monk who came to be called the father of Christian monasticism. Antony's life provided a basis for monastic thinking and practice.

We know of Antony through *The Life of Antony*, written in the fourth century by Athanasius, bishop of Alexandria. Antony's conversion highlights the role of Holy Scripture that would become a prominent feature of the Rule of Benedict.

When he was between eighteen and twenty, one Sunday morning on his way to the Lord's house Antony was pondering how in
Acts some sold all they had and placed the money at the feet of the
apostles for those in need. Just as he was walking into the church he
heard the Gospel lesson where the Lord said to the rich man, "If you
would be perfect, sell your possessions and give to the poor and you
will have treasure in heaven. Then come, follow me."[5]

Impelled by the words of scripture, Antony gave away all his possessions
and left everything behind, opting for a new way of solitude deep in the
Egyptian desert, far away from village and town. There he sought God,
pursued virtue, and, at every turn, fought the terrors of the devil. Athanasius tells amazing accounts of Antony physically battling demons, their
shrieking and attacks heard by visitors. He, of course, prevailed, becoming famous not only for his quest for perfection but also for his wisdom,
and was sought after by bishops and emperors. Athanasius shares wonderful stories about this gentle and single-minded holy man, who urged
everyone "to prefer nothing in the world above the love of Christ,"[6] an
instruction that Benedict includes in his Rule.

The Life of Antony became one of the most influential writings of
Christian history. Antony modeled a rigorous and austere discipline that,
at the time, set the terms for the Church's ideal of devotional life[7] and
inspired men and women to dedicate their lives to God. These fervent
Christians followed Antony's example and ventured deep into the desert, away from town and village, becoming Desert Fathers (Abbas) and
Mothers (Ammas). So extreme were some of their practices that during
the fourth century "there were some who believed that the true saints
were not the martyrs whose sufferings were usually brief, but the ascetics
who suffered for a whole lifetime."[8]

Benedict does not accept this pattern of suffering. While we do find
practices in Benedict's Rule that were part of Antony's discipline such as
prayer, fasting, silence, hospitality, the pursuit of virtue, and the guidance of spiritual elders, Benedict takes a more moderate approach toward

monastic life. He believes not everyone can handle the rigorous life of self-denial modeled by Antony. Benedict's more moderate approach and his preference for living in community instead of alone are what make the practices in the Rule accessible to us.

Monastic Communities Form and Leaders Emerge

Monastic communities began to form in the late third and early fourth centuries in Egypt. Just as many of us today have spiritual directors, people in the early centuries of Christianity sought out Antony and other Desert Fathers and Mothers for their wisdom and direction. These seekers often took up solitary residence near these holy men and women, forming communities where people would seek spiritual guidance and meet for prayer and the Holy Eucharist. Other Christians also ventured into the desert with the specific intention to form communities of people who were seeking God. Through both channels, monastic communities were established and took root.

Pachomius: Founder of Monastic Living in Community

Although Pachomius (290–346 CE) was not the first to establish a monastery, he is considered to be the founder of cenobitic life, the form of monastic living in community that would be favored by Benedict. "Cenobitic" comes from the Latin word *coenobium*, which means "community."

Pachomius was not born a Christian. The son of wealthy pagan parents, he was conscripted into the army as a young man. Like all new recruits, he was essentially a prisoner and was treated that way. While traveling down the Nile he spent the night at Thebes with other soldiers, locked in a prison to prevent their escape from the army. Local Christians visited the soldiers and brought them food. Impressed by such kindness, Pachomius inquired about their altruism and was told that Christians were merciful to everyone, even strangers. After hearing what a Christian was, he decided on the spot to dedicate his life to Christ.[9] (Such stories always amaze me—how quickly and easily people dedicate their lives to Christ while I struggle along, dedicating myself at one moment then retracting it the next!)

In the deserted Egyptian village of Tabennisis, shortly after being discharged from the army, Pachomius heard a voice telling him to construct a monastery there where many would come to be monks.[10] A second revelation came later through an angel who told him three times this amazing message: "Pachomius, Pachomius, the Lord's will is for you to minister to the human race and to unite them to himself."[11] Following the first command, he established a monastery. Following the second, he did everything with hearty zeal and monumental vision. He established new monasteries and brought existing ones into what he called *koinonia*, "fellowship," a Greek word drawn from the New Testament.[12] By the time of his death he headed a confederation of nine monasteries for men and two for women, together numbering over five thousand people![13]

Most early monastic communities consisted of widely dispersed cells—individual dwellings—in caves or against rocks with a central building for worship. The Pachomian monastery was a large, close complex of buildings, which became the inherited model for Benedictine monasteries. High walls were a distinctive feature; they emphasized separation from the world and offered safety. There was a gatehouse, a guest house, a kitchen, a bakery, a dining hall, an infirmary, an assembly hall (called a synaxis), and a church, in addition to houses—thirty or forty of them—where the monks lived and where each had a cell. "Later observers say that if one strolled through a Pachomian monastery, one saw an amazing variety of skilled craftsmen" such as carpenters, bakers, basket weavers, tailors, shoemakers, and blacksmiths, so that all needs could be provided within the walls.[14] The community had a leader and each house had a house master.[15] Benedict's monastics slept in dormitories rather than individual cells, but they too had leaders, called deans, for small groups of members. Benedict also instructed that all needs were to be met within the walls of the monastery.

From Pachomius Christian monasticism inherited a way to bring a collection of monasteries into a tightly regulated whole having a single head (the abbot); a single rule; a carefully ordered hierarchy of offices;

and an intricate rhythm of work, prayer, and spiritual formation. It would not be until the Middle Ages that such a vast and sophisticated organization of monastic communities would reappear but did so with the Benedictine monastery in Cluny, France, and with the Cistercian order, which we will discuss later in this introduction.[16] As a young abbot Benedict followed Pachomius's lead, although on a smaller scale, establishing twelve small monasteries of twelve monks each on a hillside in Subiaco.

Pachomius also wrote the first known monastic rule. As a speaker of Latin, Benedict would not have read this rule directly because it was written in Coptic and then translated into Greek. However, the content of the Rule of Pachomius, consisting of four books, provided a model for Basil of Caesarea, who wrote two rules that were well known to Benedict.

Basil: Champion of Scripture and Cenobitic Community

Benedict admired Basil of Caesarea (330–379 CE) and names Basil's rules as important reading in his own Rule. He includes key themes found in Basil's two rules: the primacy of scripture, the preference for cenobitic community, and the creation of a monastic organization shaped by love.

Basil established two monastic communities and became bishop of Caesarea, located on the coastal plain of present-day Israel. There had been ongoing concern about the developing monastic movement by the Church, especially toward those who journeyed to the desert to work out their own salvation through aesthetic practices. Basil realized the value of the monastic movement to the Church at a time when that very Church was in need of moral reinforcement. He also stated that the monastic movement needed "required regulation" as well as "proper surveillance" to ensure standards were established and followed if it was to be of real, permanent value to the cause of Christianity.[17]

Well-versed in Church doctrine, Basil established standards familiar to Christians even today and each finds a place in Benedict's Rule: the Bible as the guide to Christian life, the importance of keeping Jesus's commandment to love one another, the call to do God's will as a way to a deep connection with God, an emphasis on practical charity rather than extremes in fasting and other disciplines, the need for self-control, and the importance of community to represent the Body of Christ. Basil's rules stress the primacy of love—love of God and love of one's neighbor—as Jesus states in the Great Commandment (Matthew 22:37–39; Mark 12:30–31; Luke 10:27). As we will see, the emphasis on love is foremost in Benedict's Rule.

Basil believes strongly in community, a belief that Benedict readily embraces. In the solitary life Basil sees the danger of self-complacency—a monk thinking that he has already achieved the "perfect fulfillment of the commandments" when his conduct is never tested by living with others.[18] A very perceptive observation—I know my conduct is often tested and challenged by others, especially at home, and there is plenty of value in this. Benedict carries forward the emphasis of living in community not only for personal growth but also to support one another in the search for God and eternal life.

Basil's community included children—both boys and girls—who were admitted to the monastery and "trained ... in godliness" by a monk well advanced in years who showed fatherly kindness to them. Basil's rules show understanding and creativity in working with children. For example:

> Prizes will be offered for those who can best remember both words and subjects that our end may be attained with ease and pleasure to the children, and without any pain or unpleasantness. Those who are educated in this way will soon become attentive, and acquire habits of concentration.[19]

As described above, Benedict took ideas from the rules of Basil, although, to my knowledge, not the giving of prizes to children!

Later Monastic Writers Who Influenced Benedict

Beginning late in the last decade of the fourth century, other important writings influenced the content of the Rule of Benedict: a rule written by Augustine of Hippo, two documents on Egyptian monasticism by John Cassian, and the Rule of the Master.

The Rule of Augustine: Benedict's Model for Monastic Love

The monastic rule of Augustine of Hippo (354–430 CE) influenced Benedict, as seen especially in the later chapters of Benedict's Rule. Benedict must have resonated with Augustine's approach to monastic life with its emphasis on community and mutual love. In addition to his contribution to monasticism and the Rule of Benedict, Augustine became one of the greatest theologians of Western Christianity.

Born in North Africa, Augustine took to reckless living as a young man, much to the distress of his mother, Monica, who was a Christian. After following Greek philosophical thought for a number of years, he was ultimately baptized by the famous preacher Bishop Ambrose in 387 CE. Later Augustine returned to Africa, where he was ordained a priest in 391 CE and then became bishop of Hippo in 397 CE.

After his conversion to Christianity Augustine was drawn to ascetical and monastic life. When he returned to Africa he founded a monastery in Tagaste, then one in Hippo, and finally one in the church where he served as priest. Once he became bishop he turned his own household of clerics into a quasi monastery, with a common life and common ownership of property, which, one might guess, was not received warmly by all clergy. Augustine's rule, called *Praeceptum* ("teaching" or "instruction"), is brief and thought to have been written at the time he became a bishop to remind his members of what he had taught orally.[20] The most outstanding feature is the emphasis on love and community, no doubt based on the description of the early Christian community in Jerusalem found in Acts 4:32–35.

> Now the whole group of those who believed were of one heart and soul, and no one claimed private ownership of any possessions, but everything they owned was held in common. With great power the apostles gave their testimony to the resurrection of the Lord Jesus, and great grace was upon them all. There was not a needy person among them, for as many as owned lands or houses sold them and brought the proceeds of what was sold. They laid it at the apostles' feet, and it was distributed to each as any had need.

The opening of Augustine's rule presents the key features of his ideal based on scripture:

> In the first place, live together in harmony and be of one mind and heart in God; for this is the purpose of your coming together. Do not call anything your own, but hold all that you have in common; and let distribution of food and clothing be made by your superior, not to all alike, because all have not the same health, but to each according to his need. For thus you read in the Acts of the Apostles, that they had all things in common, and distribution was made to each, according as anyone had need.[21]

In his rule Augustine includes the traditional monastic practices of humility, psalmody, private prayer, *lectio divina* (prayer using Holy Scripture), fasting, silence, simplicity of food and clothing, obedience, manual labor, renunciation of property, and strict chastity.[22] Because he values community, he emphasizes the relationships of brothers to one another, as does Benedict. This focus is different from Egyptian monasticism, which was more concerned with the relationship of each individual to God as mediated through a spiritual father.[23]

Augustine's prestige as a theologian, the widespread diffusion of his writings, and finally his enthusiasm for monastic life ensured the spread of his rule within North Africa and beyond. In both Gaul and Italy, where Benedict resided, Augustine's influence upon monastic writers became so massive in the first half of the sixth century—during the time Benedict wrote his Rule—that it has been spoken of as an "Augustinian invasion."[24]

Benedict was influenced by the monastic ideals of Augustine: the importance of community and holding all possessions in common; the need for good relationships among the brothers; the distribution based on need; and the focus on love as central to monastic community, which the Rule of Augustine describes as "the very purpose of their common monastic life."[25]

The Writings of John Cassian: Chronicler of Egyptian Monasticism

Benedict received knowledge of monastic tradition not only through monastic rules but also through other foundational teachings on monasticism. The noted monk and theologian John Cassian (360–435 CE) documented the monastic tradition of Egypt in the early part of the fifth century. His writing had a deep and profound influence on Benedict. Also from a well-to-do family like Antony and Pachomius, Cassian and his friend Germanus joined a monastery in Bethlehem. They visited Egypt twice, spending as long as ten years there. Later in his life Cassian founded two monasteries in Marseilles, located in today's France, and wrote two treatises that documented what he learned as a young monk about life, worship, and spiritual practices while visiting influential Egyptian monasteries.[26]

Cassian wrote *The Conferences* as dialogues with leading Egyptian spiritual masters. This work concentrates on a person's encounter with God and is presented by Cassian, who exhibits in his writing an extensive understanding of human nature and behavior. A massive volume, *The Conferences* covers subjects such as the objective of monastic life (purity of heart) and its goal (eternal life and the kingdom of God).[27] Cassian also includes chapters on topics such as prayer, pursuing a life of virtue, forming self-knowledge, and discretion (distinguishing what is true and from God or what is false and from the devil).

The Institutes presents observations on communal life and the correction of the faults that undermine the search for God. Here Cassian again stresses the importance of moral virtue and self-knowledge. Cassian brought to Western monasticism a process for dealing with the "eight kinds of evil thoughts,"[28] created by monastic theologian Evagrius Ponticus (c. 345–399 CE) in the fourth century. These eight thoughts that can negatively influence actions are: gluttony, lust, greed, sadness, anger, *acedia* (weariness of soul or distain), vanity, and pride.

Later *acedia* was removed, and the list became known as the "Seven Deadly Sins."

Cassian's work was invaluable in disseminating Egyptian monastic tradition in the West. While Benedict does not quote Cassian's actual words, his Rule reflects Cassian's work, thus honoring and embracing Egyptian monastic ideals. Benedict also includes *The Conferences* and *The Institutes* as recommended reading in chapter 73 of the Rule, reflecting the importance of following monastic tradition.

The Rule of the Master: A Primary Resource for the Rule of Benedict

The Rule of the Master was Benedict's main written resource from which he drew extensive text. Yet, as we will see, Benedict liberally modified the Master's rule in order to express his own vision of monastic life.

The Rule of the Master is about three times longer than the Rule of Benedict and is thought to have been written in the sixth century before Benedict wrote his own Rule. The Master, an abbot unknown by name, is extremely thorough in his approach to all aspects of monastic life, down to the minutest detail. This includes such topics as leadership in the monastery; the liturgy; the practice of humility; how the monks were to spend their days; and copious instructions concerning punishment, living arrangements, meals, dress, and so forth.

Although the Master is interested in the souls of the monks, to me, his zeal to keep them from sin results in an approach more akin to the eye of a watchdog waiting for a fault to be revealed. A disobedient monk is reported to the abbot; named "a servant of the devil," "a scab in the flock," and "an enemy of God" (wow!); and subjected to a lengthy verbal chastisement by the abbot followed by excommunication (enforced separation from the others for work and meals).[29] Yet in all fairness, the Master is not unkind in other matters, stating that "delicate and weak brothers should be assigned such work as will nourish them for the service of God, not kill them."[30]

In drawing from the Rule of the Master, Benedict leaves out material that does not fit with his view of community and leadership or that he considers punitive, such as the watchdog approach to discipline described above. He offers a more moderate approach to monastic life and removes much of the minutia found in the Master's rule. He adds new material he feels is important, such as the qualities monastic leaders should possess and how the members of the monastery are to treat one another.

Several years ago I did a fascinating comparison of the Rule of the Master and the Rule of Benedict. This study gave me a glimpse into Benedict's character and what he saw as important in monastic life. The first seven chapters of Benedict's Rule are literally copied from the Rule of the Master, with modifications. Chapters 8 through 67 in Benedict's Rule take some text from the Rule of the Master but with significant modifications. Finally, the last six chapters have little or no relationship at all to the Rule of the Master. Here Benedict adds chapters that were totally missing from the Rule of the Master but that are in line with Augustinian thought. Benedict is a masterful synthesizer of monastic tradition, written text, and personal vision.

The Life of Benedict

In addition to being influenced by monastic writings and traditions, Benedict was influenced by the times in which he lived. His world was in the throes of upheaval, instability, and danger. Rome had fallen in 410 CE. The last Roman emperor, Romulus, was deposed in 476 CE, four years before Benedict's birth. Barbarians such as the Huns and the Vandals had invaded. After a brief time of peace under the Ostrogoth king Theodoric, warfare began again in 526 CE. High culture collapsed, injustice prevailed. The Church was distracted by the fury of theological controversies. In this chaotic and dangerous world Benedict wrote a Rule that promised a just, well-ordered, and Christ-centered life.

Our only source of information about Benedict—other than the Rule itself—is the second book of the *Dialogues* written in 593–594 CE by Gregory the Great, the first Benedictine pope. Gregory based his work on the testimony of four monks who knew Benedict. Gregory's work is not a biography as we know today but a literary form called hagiography, a way of writing about the lives of saints that focuses on wondrous accounts of miracles and stories. While possibly basing these stories on some level of fact, Gregory's main purpose was to edify, inspire, and provide encouragement to his beleaguered flock, who felt that God had abandoned them in an unstable and violent time.

Benedict Turns Toward God and Is Tempted Three Times

Gregory begins the life of Benedict with these words: "There was a man whose life was worthy of veneration, Benedict by name and blessed by grace."[31]

Benedict was born in 480 CE in Nursia, Italy, today called Norcia, which is about sixty miles northeast of Rome. His family had sent him to Rome to study for a liberal education. Noticing how many students fell headlong into vice and wishing to please God alone, he left home and studies "in search of the habit of a holy way of life."[32]

Early in Gregory's account, Benedict overcame three temptations, each resulting in an increase in both virtue and service to others. The first temptation came when his prayer mended a broken sieve. People were in awe and hung the sieve at the entrance of the church. Benedict secretly fled, wanting to work only for God and not for the praise of people. For three years he lived alone in a cramped cave in Subiaco, a remote place about forty miles from Rome. A monk named Romanus from a nearby monastery discovered Benedict and smuggled bread to him from his personal rations.

Benedict's next temptation came in a vision of a woman setting his soul on fire and causing him to consider abandoning the wilderness. Gregory describes the graphic refusal of this temptation.

> Suddenly he was touched by heavenly grace and came to himself once more. Seeing some dense bushes with nettles and brambles growing nearby, he took off his clothes and threw himself naked into those sharp thorns and stinging nettles [!].... Rolling around in them for a long time [!!].... As temptation receded then, the man of God produced a more abundant harvest of virtues....[33]

Benedict became famous as word of his exemplary life of virtue spread among the people. Members of a nearby monastery asked him to be their abbot. Benedict reluctantly accepted, warning them that his way of life would not suit them. The inevitable happened—it did not work out. What to do to free themselves of this unreasonable abbot, the disgruntled monks pondered? They decided to poison his wine. When Benedict blessed this wine at the meal, which is the monastic custom, the goblet broke. Understanding then that the wine had been poisoned, Benedict grieved, "May God almighty have pity on you, my brothers.... Did I not say to you at the beginning that your ways and mine were incompatible?"[34] Once again Benedict was victorious over this third temptation because instead of being angry and vengeful, he was forgiving.

Benedict wisely left that monastery and established twelve monasteries on a hillside in Subiaco, each housing twelve monks and an abbot. As these communities flourished, Benedict also inspired many people outside the monastery to be "fervent in their love of the Lord God, Jesus Christ."[35] But the demon of jealousy reared its head in a local priest, Florentius, who was smitten with envy at Benedict's holiness and his influence on the people. What to do to get the praise being heaped upon the man of God? He sent bread to the holy abbot that Benedict recognized as poisoned. Holding the bread in his hand Benedict instructed the raven who always came to receive bread from him, "In the name of the Lord Jesus Christ, take this bread and drop it somewhere where no one can find it," which is exactly what the raven did.[36] Benedict grieved for this jealous monk more than for himself.

Undaunted and burning with a desire to be free of Benedict, Florentius tried again, this time sending seven naked girls into the garden of Benedict's cell to dance before him. Unfazed, Benedict was more concerned about the young monastics, who could easily succumb to this temptation. Again, Benedict moved on. As a postscript to this story, we read that while standing on a terrace celebrating Benedict's departure, the terrace collapsed, killing Florentius.[37]

Monte Cassino and the Birth of Benedict's Rule

Benedict journeyed to a place called Monte Cassino, about eighty miles south of Rome, where he established a monastery. It was at Monte Cassino that Benedict lived out his life as abbot and wrote the Rule for his community. Just like his Rule reaches out to teach us today, Benedict's influence extended beyond the monastic walls of Monte Cassino to the large number of non-Christians in the area. Gregory writes, "By preaching ceaselessly he called to the faith all those living in the vicinity."[38] Gregory shares many stories of miracles and prophecies that were birthed in this place. Here is one ...

Benedict had a sister, Scholastica, a nun who had been dedicated to the Lord since infancy. Scholastica visited her brother once a year, meeting in a building far below the monastery, the latter being on an imposing hill. One day when Scholastica had come for this visit, she and her brother praised God together and talked of holy things. After sharing a meal, Scholastica said, "'I beg you not to leave me tonight, so that we might talk until morning about the joys of the heavenly life.' Benedict answered her, 'What are you saying, sister? I certainly cannot stay away from my monastery.'"[39] Gregory continues:

> The sky was so clear at the time that there was not a cloud to be seen. When the nun heard the words of her brother's refusal she put her hands together on the table and bent her head in her hands to pray to the almighty Lord. When she lifted her head from the table, such violent lightning and thunder burst forth, together with a great downpour of rain, that neither the venerable Benedict nor the brothers who were with him could set foot outside the door of the place where they were sitting. For the nun, as she bent her head in her hands, had poured forth tears on to the table, by means of which she had turned the clear sky into rain.[40]

Benedict was not happy and asked God to forgive his sister. But realizing that he could not return, he and Scholastica talked of holy things throughout the night. Gregory explains that Benedict was able to see how God was moved by a woman's heart. Three days later Benedict "raised his eyes to heaven and saw the soul of his sister: it had departed from her body and penetrated the mysterious regions of heaven in the form of a dove."[41]

On another occasion we read that Benedict was gifted with a vision, the whole world drawn together beneath a single ray of sunlight. In its midst he saw the soul of Germanus, the bishop of Capua, being carried up to heaven by the angels in a fiery sphere.[42]

In 547 CE Benedict became ill, gripped by a high fever that grew worse every day. On the sixth day he made his disciples carry him into the chapel. After taking the Lord's body and blood in Holy Communion, while his disciples supported his weak body, "he stood with his hands raised to heaven and breathed his last in the middle of a prayer."[43] A beautiful picture of the end, and the new beginning, of this holy man's journey of faith.

Forty years after Benedict's death his monastery at Monte Cassino was destroyed by the barbarian Lombards, a reality that Benedict had seen in a vision before he died. This monastery was rebuilt and destroyed twice more, the final time during World War II. Today, rebuilt and functioning, the monastery at Monte Cassino is a destination for Benedictine pilgrims. Where his relics lie is a matter of dispute. The abbey at Monte Cassino claims this privilege but so does the abbey of St. Benôit-sur-Loire in France.

History of the Rule After the Time of Benedict

In the early centuries following Benedict's death, the Rule spread gradually through missionary works of monks such as Augustine of Canterbury, who was sent to England in 595 CE by Gregory the Great. In the eighth century a monk named Benedict of Aniane (750–821 CE) adopted Benedict's Rule for his monastery in order to reform monasticism, which had become prosperous but worldly over the centuries. In 792 CE, Charlemagne (Charles the Great) took this "Second Benedict's" monastery under royal protection. Monks were sent to other monasteries. Through Benedict of Aniane's efforts every monastic custom within these monasteries was measured against the Rule of Benedict, the *una regula*, "the one rule" as it was named by this Benedict.[44] A standard observance using the Rule in France and Germany came through two synods of abbots held in 816 CE and 817 CE, making the Rule obligatory for all monks in the empire.

Monastic reforms in the West continued throughout the next several centuries in various parts of what is today Europe, which further expanded the use of Benedict's Rule. Benedictines brought both Christianity and civilization to much of Europe. As Esther de Waal describes it, "In a world in which barbarian invasion, political uncertainty, and the power of the sword seemed the most immediate realities ... the monasteries came to stand out as centres of light and learning."[45]

Benedict became the patriarch of Western monasticism and his Rule the most influential in the Western Church. By the high Middle Ages (eleventh through thirteenth centuries), most of the monasteries in the West had adopted his Rule. One of the most famous was Cluny in Burgundy, France, a powerful and wealthy abbey that became the mother abbey of other dependent priories and reformed monasteries. Cluny was most admired for its elaborate liturgy of the Divine Office sung in a church building cited as one of the marvels of Christendom.[46]

Reacting to the excesses of powerful monastic houses such as Cluny, some monks sought to return to a faithful following of the Rule. A reformed monastery was founded at Cîteaux and the Cistercian order was born. Under the famous abbot and writer Bernard of Clairvaux, who arrived at Cîteaux in 1112 CE, many daughter houses were founded, totaling 339 at Bernard's death. They named themselves "schools of charity," where one could learn the secrets of both divine love and mutual love among the brothers,[47] echoing two themes from Benedict's Rule—the search for God and the importance of love. Abbots from these monasteries met to reflect on their faithfulness in following the Rule in order to promote a common understanding of it.[48]

Challenges and Growth and More Challenges

After the golden age of the Rule in the eleventh and twelfth centuries, the following centuries brought many challenges to Benedictine monasticism and the Rule. Although at a low point in the thirteenth century and challenged by the new Franciscans and Dominican orders, Benedictinism and the Rule did not disappear. A great flowering of reform movements in the fifteenth century was followed by the destruction of half the monasteries during the Protestant Reformation.[49] The tide began to turn several centuries later in the nineteenth century. Reform and renewal created a new type of Benedictine life that looked back to the Middle Ages as a new beginning.

Most Benedictine and Cistercian houses today owe their origins to efforts in the nineteenth century. These Benedictine houses ensured that the Rule would be influential in continuing to shape monastic life.[50] Monasteries were established for Protestants, unthinkable at any previous time since the Reformation, led by the Anglican Church in the 1840s. By the end of the century the Benedictine Confederation was formed to join monasteries in a loose international union of houses that follow the Benedictine Rule.

Although some communities were established earlier, monasteries guided by the Rule came to America in earnest through the efforts of existing European monastic houses in countries such as Germany, Switzerland, and England. The first American Benedictine monastery for men was established in 1846 in Latrobe, Pennsylvania. In the 1850s a monastery for women was established in St. Mary, Pennsylvania. From these houses and others Benedictine life spread throughout the country. By the end of the nineteenth century the Rule was guiding the lives of women and men in many Benedictine houses. While over fifty monasteries were established in the twentieth century in the United States, the greatest growth has been outside the United States in areas such as Africa.

Vatican II (1962–65), an assembly of Roman Catholic religious leaders, brought an important period of renewal in monastic life, calling for a return to ancient sources like Basil and Cassian discussed earlier. Reforms included an evaluation of monastic spirituality in light of the contemporary world. As of the middle of the twentieth century, Benedictine women and men have been active in interreligious dialogue with Buddhist, Hindu, Muslim, and Jewish communities. Frère Christian de Chergé, a French Trappist monk, reminds us that "To speak of God in another way is not to speak of another God."[51]

"Monastic history is full of ups and downs," reflects Fr. Michael Casey, a Benedictine monk, scholar, and author living in Australia. In a statement that reveals important themes in the Rule, Casey continues: "It will always be a corporate form of truly seeking God in a lifestyle that is ordinary, obscure and laborious, lived in the hope that in all things God may be glorified. Amen!"[52]

Importance of Monasticism to Christianity

How has the Rule and the monastic lifestyle been important to Christianity? Monasticism and monastic communities were birthed through the Church and became places where the teachings of Jesus centered around spiritual practices.

The Rule of Benedict helped the monastic communities form deep roots in the disciplines of prayer, silence, and worship, as well as in living the gospel life in community, seeking God, and serving one another. As the Church grew, theologians sought to clarify beliefs about God, Jesus, the Trinity, sin, and so forth. Benedictines were aware of these theological writings but instead concentrated on the practical application of scriptural principles in order to reach unity with God. Monastics of Benedict's day were expected to have some knowledge of letters (writing and reading) and an understanding of doctrine but this would not be separate from the spiritual quest. The search for God was primarily based on experience.[53] All reading, all learning was directed toward the monastic goal of eternal life. With a focus on practice, the Rule is not doctrine or a theological document. The Rule is a compendium of how to live a life that is focused on seeking God in community. Whether or not we worship in a way that reflects the liturgical practices of the Rule, "all of us share, in various forms, the practice of prayer and contemplation that is rooted in monastic tradition."[54]

The Rule is important also because monastic living is Christian living intensified. Totally dedicated to God in the choice of lifestyle and shaped by the Rule, monastic women and men are like beacons pointing us to what is truly important at the core of our being—to seek the presence of God in our lives, strive to live a life of compassion and wholeness, and become the person that we are meant to be in God's wisdom. Finally, important forms of prayer such as *lectio divina* (prayer using Holy Scripture) and centering prayer have been preserved through the monastic community and the Rule and offered to Christians outside the enclosure of the monastery.

The Benedictine way of life continues to be influential in the lives of Christians and non-Christians. Many monasteries today offer a place for people like you and me to step away from the busyness of our lives, to take part in the rhythm of daily life that shapes Benedictine men and women, to learn about the Rule, and to experience peace, rest, and renewal. Spending time in a monastery can change how we look at life. The Rule stresses moderation, so living quarters are simple—a small room, a twin bed, a desk and chair, and perhaps a more comfortable chair to sit in for reading or prayer. Arriving at home after a retreat years ago, I recall being overwhelmed with the amount of stuff that was in my house!

Benedict's Rule—A Living and Relevant Guide

Benedict inherited a centuries-old monastic tradition as we discussed earlier. He had a profound knowledge of this tradition, not of the academic type but an understanding of its truth that comes through years of *lectio divina* and immersion in both the Word of God (scripture) and the writings of the holy catholic Fathers.[55] Benedict gained his incredible knowledge of monastic tradition through experience—living the monastic life as monk and leader.

Benedict as Synthesizer of Monastic Tradition

Benedict's clear and broad vision and liberal attitude of mind brought together different branches of the monastic tradition in a harmony that sets his Rule apart from the other Latin rules. As an example, he used text and practices from the Rule of the Master and its Egyptian tradition but simplified and then softened them with the traditions of Basil and Augustine.[56]

So masterfully did he weave various sources, it is often difficult to pinpoint which exact source he actually used for specific Rule passages. Since Benedict appears not to have copied verbatim from Cassian, did Cassian's thought in the Rule come through Benedict copying the Master's rule or is it a paraphrase of Cassian's work penned by Benedict? Some of the contact Benedict had with sources "was not direct but at second or even third hand."[57] Monastic writers borrowed from one another, interested more in the truth and the value of each practice and less in knowing (or caring) who first formulated it in a particular way.[58] I will add that they also were not bound by copyright law!

Free from a narrow viewpoint and passing over transient details, Benedict's Rule eventually "was recognized as the finest expression of monastic tradition the Western experience had produced, and it gradually came to supplant all the others ... [as] the most complete and masterful synthesis of monastic tradition."[59]

The Rule of Benedict: A Guide for Christian Living

The Latin word we translate as "rule" is *regula*, which is not a law but a standard. Everything in the Rule points to Benedict's overarching theme: the standards he feels are needed to seek God and salvation in loving community.

Originally written in Latin, Benedict's Rule has an introductory Prologue and seventy-three chapters, each with a title that explains the majority of the content within that chapter, such as "Qualities of the Abbot or Prioress," "Reverence in Prayer," "The Reception of Guests," and "Distribution of Goods According to Need." Please do not be intimidated by the number of chapters; one contemporary translation is only about the size of a checkbook. In modern translations such as the one I am using for these selections, each chapter is sequentially numbered and, like the Bible, includes verse numbers. In my annotations I show Rule references like this: RB 4.15, which means Rule of Benedict, chapter 4, verse 15.

A few words about the content of the Rule may be helpful to give you a framework before we get into the annotations. I see four broad categories within the Rule:

Liturgical Instructions for the Divine Office, or *Opus Dei* ("the work of God"). These are the eight daily community prayer services that are the main occupation of the monastics.

Roles, Responsibilities, and Procedures for Community Members. Benedict provides specific instructions for jobs within the community such as for the abbot (in a male monastery) or prioress or abbess (in a female monastery), who are the superiors of the monastery; the cellarer, who distributes food and utensils to the monastics; and the porter, who greets visitors at the gate of the monastery. But Benedict's main concern is with the personal qualities needed by each person and how he or she is to treat others. Benedict's focus is on *being* rather than *doing*, which is why this Rule is helpful to us as well.

How to Live Together in Community. An important focus of the Rule involves relationships: how members should treat one another and conduct themselves to promote peace and harmony in the community and support one another. Again, we can bring his practical instructions into our lives as we seek to promote peace and harmony where we are. Addressing logistical matters in community, Benedict also includes directions for such things as sleeping arrangements, meals, food, clothing, work, discipline, and the process for joining the monastery.

Spiritual Direction. Benedict encourages monastics to take their relationship with God seriously and actively nurture it. He provides directions for such disciplines as prayer, study, Lenten practices, and living with humility before God.[60]

Here is one of my favorite descriptions of the content of the Rule from Anglican scholar Esther de Waal:

> It is all about love.
> It points me to Christ.
> Ultimately the whole meaning and purpose of the Rule is simply, [in Benedict's own words] "Prefer nothing to the love of Christ."[61]

Following the importance of scripture in monastic tradition, the Rule is permeated with and shaped by Holy Scripture. The Psalms, Proverbs, the Gospels, and selected letters of Paul are Benedict's main scriptural authorities. He draws from and quotes them continually as he explains the way of life that will bring his community closer to God. He gives practical and concrete ways to follow the teachings of scripture, especially how we are to conduct ourselves and how we are to treat other people. Jesus says, "Just as I have loved you, you also should love one another" (John 13:34). Benedict shows us how to bring this love alive. As Cistercian monk Andre Louf explains, "Benedict wrote the Rule from his own personal experience and in doing so he filled the words of his book with life, for he filled them with the knowledge that comes from living."[62] The Rule has never been a "dead letter"[63] but contains life within itself for anyone who truly listens to it.

The Rule was originally written by Benedict for his community of men. For centuries women of the Benedictine order heard only male images of brother and abbot and so felt distanced from their own tradition. Because I understand and relate to their experience and believe that other readers of this book may as well, I chose to use an inclusive language version of the Rule based on the well-known contemporary translation *RB1980: The Rule of St. Benedict in English*. Offered by the Benedictine Sisters of Erie in 1989, *A Reader's Version of the Rule of Saint Benedict in Inclusive Language* does not change the Rule but gives a reading that all of us—women and men alike—can find rich and accessible. This translation is also used in Sr. Joan Chittister's thoughtful and inspiring commentary on the Rule, *The Rule of Benedict: A Spirituality for the 21st Century,* cited in this book.

The Value of the Rule of Benedict

The success of the Rule is due to its own innate qualities of flexibility; it does not legislate short-lived and detailed requirements drawn up for a specific place and time that would make it ultimately obsolete.[64] Benedict's process of synthesizing tradition and simplifying a monastic rule has made it possible for each generation of monastic women and men to view the Rule with new eyes.

> No single generation of monks or nuns can exhaust all its riches.... Each epoch and each church brings forth that form of monastic life which best expresses its own grace.[65]

The ability to bring a spiritual experience has also enabled the Rule to remain living and vital over the centuries.[66] André Louf, a former abbot of the Cistercian Abbey of Mont-des-Cats, writes:

> A reform is only a new re-reading of the text. This modern word "re-reading" describes well what happens as each generation of monks [and women monastics] takes up the Rule anew. The text passes from one generation to another, from hand to hand and from heart to heart. Gradually and imperceptibly all its potential and depth are brought to light.[67]

That I am writing this book and that you have chosen to read it places us both within a tradition that gained momentum in the twentieth century—the use of the Rule of Benedict outside the monastic community. People recognize that the Rule can help form a compassionate heart that is so needed in today's world of competition, consumerism, and complacency. Many people find that Benedict's voice speaks to them, giving inspiration and guidance in their search for God and for a life beyond the superficial. Individuals and even families become associated with Benedictine monasteries as oblates (associates in some monasteries) to enrich their Christian way of life.

A Closing Thought

Benedict's message of moderation, balance, living in the present moment, and finding the sacred in the ordinary offers a countercultural approach to life in the twenty-first century. Episcopal priest, author, and retreat leader Elizabeth Canham writes:

> I fell in love because this man spoke of a life in a hospitable community, of simplicity, balance, and an ordered way of living designed to create an environment that fosters freedom to grow fully into the persons God created us to be.[68]

For those of us who are Christian, the Rule shows practical and doable ways that we can live the covenant made at our baptism—to seek Christ and serve others.

As you explore the practices found in the Rule, I invite you to take a small part that resonates with you and live this in your life. Even if you do not like rules, I truly hope you grow to like *this* Rule!

The Rule of
Benedict

1 Listen! The very first word of Benedict's Rule announces what is important for both the monastic and Christian. "For Benedict, listening is the fundamental attitude from which all other attitudes flow" (Böckmann). We are to listen with all of our being, from the heart, the center of life where we touch God and where God's love touches us. Benedict asks us to be silent, quieting our busy minds and furtive actions, and to listen attentively to the Rule as a guide to action.

2 Faithfulness is a theme we encounter throughout the Rule. It is an expression of stability, one of the vows that a monk, brother, nun, or sister takes in the Benedictine tradition. Stability means remaining faithful to people and place as well as to God.

Throughout this book monastics will be referred to as monks, brothers, nuns or sisters. Nuns generally remain cloistered in the monastery and sisters engage in work outside the monastic community. In our American culture the terms *nun* and *sister* are often interchanged.

≈ God speaks to us in many different ways: through scripture, this Rule, the circumstances of our lives, family, friends, church and other communities, books, nature, our joys, and our sorrows. We are to listen wholeheartedly by being present in the moment, yet listening is one of the most difficult things to do. When I am speaking to another person, I often catch myself thinking about what I am going to say next, or I am judging the person because I do not agree with what he or she is saying. I might even be planning dinner! This is not listening. As the one who loves us, Benedict asks for our complete attention.

1 □ Opening Our Eyes to the Light from God

The Prologue to the Rule

The compelling Prologue introduces important themes in the Rule—listening, obedience to Christ, the urgency of seeking God and salvation, actions that will foster love and amend our faults, and reliance on God's grace. As you read, notice Benedict's use of scripture to present and reinforce the ideas. Key Benedictine practices appear in the first four verses: to listen, to take willing action, to give up self-will for Christ, and to pray.

Listen carefully, my child, to my instructions, and attend to them with the ear of your heart.[1] This is advice from one who loves you; welcome it, and faithfully put it into practice.[2]

PROLOGUE 1

3 Obedience is another Benedictine vow. Benedictine obedience is *listening and responding*—to listen by being present to a person or in a situation, and then to take action, as Benedict instructs in Prologue 1. He lets us know that obedience takes work.

4 The monastic is to be obedient to the Rule, the abbot or prioress, and the community. Here I believe that you and I are not so different from Benedict's monks. We too can be lazy in pursuing a relationship with God, drifting away so subtly that we are not even aware we have moved until we have gone quite far. Disobedience is focusing so much on our desires, plans, and activities that we have no thought or time to be aware of God's direction.

5 Giving up self-will for God's will is a key concept in the monastic journey and a goal for the monastic as well as for any Christian. This action frees us to give our whole self to God. Benedict asks for a full and final commitment to this. We can do the same *if* we are ready.

6 The Latin word here, *militatarus*, also means "service."

7 The Rule is Christocentric, centered in Christ. Benedict does not speak of the earthly Jesus but of the risen Christ.

∿ Human will can motivate both good and evil. While we can never really give up our *whole* will, we can exchange the self-centered and self-destructive parts for the life-giving will of God. For example, my self-will may urge me to flee from a complaining friend but God's will asks for compassion and a listening ear. And it *is* a battle!

The labor of obedience[3] will bring you back to God from whom you had drifted through the sloth of disobedience.[4]

PROLOGUE 2

This message of mine is for you, then, if you are ready to give up your own will, once and for all,[5] and armed with the strong and noble weapons of obedience to do battle[6] for Jesus, the Christ.[7]

PROLOGUE 3

8 As a first step toward obedience, in Prologue 4 Benedict says, "Pray!" Through prayer we express our intention to turn from self-will. This is *not* a prayer of perfectionism. An alternative translation is to "bring it to completion"; to allow God to work through us toward God's plan, which may very well be different from our own. By calling on God for help, Benedict makes it clear that he does not align his Rule with Pelagianism, the fifth-century heresy that divine aid was unnecessary and we humans could choose good over evil. *Ora et labora*, prayer and work, is often used to describe the Benedictine way.

≈ Beginning every task with prayer is a spiritual discipline that I try to do. It is difficult to remember, especially as I tend to rush into a task or jump from one task to another. Yet, when I remember, prayer promotes greater calm and thoughtfulness as I work because I've opened my heart to God. Try this practice.

9 In other translations of the Rule, *dominus,* translated here as "God," is often rendered "Lord," and can be interpreted as "Christ." Benedict makes little distinction between Christ and the Father (Kardong).

10 Although many of us may find this picture of God disturbing, Benedict reveals in the Rule that he sees the final judgment as a reality. Yet he continually points to the light of God. Both the monastic and Christian can choose a life that leads to eternal punishment or to glory. Benedict may have borrowed this image from Roman life—a son does not need to work, but is to show his father love by obeying him and not causing him distress (Böckmann). To be punished was to lose the security of the family, which was to lose all security and, literally, to lose your life (Chittister). We are already God's children, given gifts to be used in life-giving ways as an expression of our obedience. I think Benedict would approve of bestselling author and Benedictine sister Joan Chittister's explanation of these verses: "We have been loved to life by God, and now we must love God back with our whole lives or forever live a living death" (Chittister).

First of all, every time you begin a good work, you must pray to God most earnestly to bring it to perfection.[8]

PROLOGUE 4

In God's goodness, we are already counted as God's own, and therefore we should never grieve the Holy One by our evil actions. With the good gifts which are in us, we must obey God at all times that God[9] may never become the angry parent who disinherits us, nor the dreaded one, enraged by our sins, who punishes us forever as worthless servants for refusing to follow the way to glory.[10]

PROLOGUE 5–7

---

11 Psalm 95 is sung every morning in Benedictine communities, reminding the monastics that it is not for themselves alone that they listen; they listen for ways to serve others. Notice how Benedict uses Holy Scripture from Paul's Letter to the Romans to sound an urgent call for us to wake up and be attentive to God.

> Being hard of heart can be connected with sleeping, laziness, and insensitivity ... yet the heart can also be hardened in refusal and pride. We may deliberately plug up our ears and let everything slide off us. Perhaps we fear the consequences of what we hear. Here, however, it is not the voice of a tyrant but that of a loving and inviting Lord (Prologue 19), though we may harden our heart precisely against love and choose to remain frozen and be left alone. (Böckmann)

Prologue 10 includes Benedict's second mention of the heart.

12 What is the message from the Spirit? To reverence God, which is the foundation of the spiritual life and "one of Benedict's key spiritual ideas" (Kardong). Other translations may use "fear," which is not being terror-stricken but having reverent awe of God's power and majesty where love is a result.

13 Here the word "walk," found in scripture, has been replaced by the more urgent "run." Be on the lookout for three more uses of "run" in the Prologue.

〜 Every day the voice from heaven calls out to us through our interactions with people, what we are responsible for, what we read, what we see, and what we are asked to do. Will we recognize the urgency of our response, soften our hearts, and take action?

14 The five scripture passages found in Prologue 8–13 reinforce the call to action, a theme in the Rule. Benedict fills these inspiring verses with energetic verbs: "get up," "rouse," "arise," "listen," "run." Benedict's community is to be on the move, seeking God and eternal life. No

(continued on page 10)

Let us get up then, at long last, for the Scriptures rouse us when they say: "It is high time for us to arise from sleep" (Rom. 13:11). Let us open our eyes to the light that comes from God, and our ears to the voice from the heavens that every day calls out this charge: "If you hear God's voice today, do not harden your hearts" (Ps. 95:8).[11] And again: "You that have ears to hear, listen to what the Spirit says to the churches" (Rev. 2:7). And what does the Spirit say? "Come and listen to me; I will teach you to reverence God"[12] (Ps. 34:12). Run[13] "while you have the light of life, that the darkness of death may not overtake you" (John 12:35).

PROLOGUE 8–13[14]

dallying here! Notice how many times Benedict speaks of God's call and our listening. Benedictine nun and scholar Sister Aquinata Böckmann writes:

> From its first word almost to its end, the Prologue is permeated by listening: to the word, to the presence of God, obedience to him, doing the good that grows out of obeying/listening, fighting against what is negative, and finally running on the way while listening to the Gospel. (Böckmann)

Prologue 8–13 begins the prolific use of scripture found throughout the Rule. Watch how Benedict uses scripture to give authority to what he's saying and asking of his community.

15   God seeks workers, not just for a task but also to bring them life and good days. This is indeed a stunning offer to Benedict's community as well as to us.

16   Choice is another theme in the Rule, highlighted in the Prologue by Benedict's use of the word "if."

17   *If* we desire life that has meaning and worth beyond the narrow confines of self-interest there is a certain way we are to live. Continuing his use of Psalm 34, Benedict points us to actions that will promote peace in relationships and community. While Benedict would not have read *Sayings of the Desert Fathers*, he inherited the traditions of these early monastics and so would have nodded a hearty consent to this story:

> The brothers bring a parchment to Abbot Abraham and ask him to write a long text. But he writes only the one verse of Psalm 34:15, "Avoid evil and do good, seek peace and pursue it." The brothers say: "Please write the entire psalm." But he answers: "When you will have conformed your entire life to the precept of this one verse, then I will write another text down for you." (Böckmann)

Seeking workers in a multitude of people, God calls out and says again: "Is there anyone here who yearns for life and desires to see good days?" (Ps. 34:13).[15] If you hear this and your answer is "I do,"[16] God then directs these words to you: If you desire true and eternal life, "keep your tongue free from vicious talk and your lips from all deceit; turn away from evil and do good; let peace be your quest and aim" (Ps. 34:14–15).[17]

PROLOGUE 14–17

〜 Do you yearn for a way of life that can bring joy and good days? I sure do. The way to both, Benedict explains, is by being people of peace in our relationships.

In our personal universe we have so many opportunities to be for peace, to speak for peace, and to act for peace. The Benedictine community is shaped by Christ and centered in Christ so that all seek to continually return to him and support one another in this quest. When we live by Benedictine values, even if you and I are the only ones doing this, we can still become a catalyst for positive and life-giving change within our communities and relationships. (Tomaine)

You will see throughout the Rule how Benedict structures work, informs leadership, and builds relationships that will help create an environment of harmony and peace in the monastery.

18 Here God is doing the listening. Once we have begun to turn from evil, do good, and seek peace, we lower the barriers between us and God. We become better able to hear God's direction.

19 "Sweeter" is an alternate translation. "God is the food for adults, and what they receive from God is always divine, is always sweet (1 Peter 2:3)" (Böckmann).

20 Benedict closes this opening part of the Prologue with a statement of joy that God's initiative seeks us out and offers us life and love, now!

〜 Prologue 18–20, wonderfully hope-filled, assures us of God's presence and how God reaches out to us to show us the way. What *could* be more delightful? Benedict knows the joy that comes from obedience to Christ. I believe that Benedict is also aware of how difficult it is to seek peace. He wants to give encouragement to those of us who say "I do" to God's call.

Once you have done this, my "eyes will be upon you and my ears will listen for your prayers; and even before you ask me, I will say" to you: "Here I am" (Isa. 58:9).[18] What is more delightful[19] than this voice of the Holy One calling to us? See how God's love shows us the way of life.[20]

PROLOGUE 18–20

21 Prologue 21 contains four important themes found in the Rule: faith, good works in service of others, the Gospel as guide, and the goal of salvation. Benedict encourages the monastics to begin the journey.

22 Here is the fifth occurrence of "if" thus far in the Prologue. For Benedict, having life and good days is not a done deal; action is required to be in God's tent, God's kingdom here on earth where God is always present.

23 The urgency continues as Benedict uses the verb "run." No time is to be wasted.

〜 At Prologue 23 Benedict begins a section using Psalm 15 to explain the actions of those who will dwell in God's kingdom and God's role in this. The question-and-answer format was frequently used in monastic writings where elders teach disciples.

24 Benedict often calls the Psalmist "the prophet" although he doubtless considers King David the author of the Psalms (Kardong).

Clothed then with faith and the performance of good works, let us set out on this way, with the Gospel for our guide, that we may deserve to see the Holy One "who has called us to the eternal presence" (1 Thess. 2:12).[21] If we wish to dwell in God's tent,[22] we will never arrive unless we run there by doing good deeds.[23]

PROLOGUE 21–22

But let us ask with the prophet:[24] "Who will dwell in your tent, O God; who will find rest upon your holy mountain?" (Ps. 15:1). After this question, then, let us listen well to what God says in reply, for we are shown the way to God's tent.

PROLOGUE 23–24

25 Once again, the heart is the source of action. See Prologue 1 and 10, and notes 1 and 11.

26 In earlier monasticism living an ascetic life was considered to be the highest form of spiritual practice. Benedict's monks lived in community, and so creating loving and respectful relationships was the criteria for holiness.

27 Also translated "away from the sight of his heart" (Böckmann), which again emphasizes the importance that Benedict places on the heart. "The devil wants to get close to the heart. He attacks the center of a person very gently so that, at the beginning, we may not notice it or even see the attack as something good" (Böckmann). Oh, how true!

28 From the time of early Christian monasticism, self-awareness was critical to spiritual growth. Men and women sought to identify unhelpful or damaging thoughts at their rising so that they would not trigger negative or destructive actions. Benedict uses physically strong verbs: "flinging," "catching hold of," and "dashing" against Christ. The latter is a reference to Psalm 137, where revenge is taken by throwing infants upon rocks.

〜 In discussing Prologue 28 at retreats and workshops, most people are shocked and offended at the violent image of dashing temptations against Christ. To me, the image illustrates Benedict's conviction that the evil one—the devil—is a serious threat; only Christ can help us overcome this threat. How might we shatter these thoughts against Christ when we recognize them? Sharing them with a trusted spiritual guide or friend is one way, or handing these thoughts to Jesus and letting him carry them away. Another way is to find a symbol for the thought or obsession, like a rock or an acorn, and fling it into the woods.

29 Benedict is clear in Prologue 29–30 that good works are the result of God's action, once again countering the Pelagian heresy. See Prologue 4 and note 8 above.

〜 Do you feel pleased when you've helped another person or done a task well? I do. Let's always remember to turn to God, giving thanks and praise for the inspiration and ability that made our actions fruitful.

"Those who walk without blemish and are just in all
dealings; who speak truth from the heart[25] and have not
practiced deceit; who have not wronged another in any way,
not listened to slanders against a neighbor" (Ps. 15:2–3).[26]
They have foiled the evil one at every turn, flinging both the
devil and these wicked promptings far from sight.[27] While
these temptations were still "young, the just caught hold of
them and dashed them against" Christ (Ps. 15:4, 137:9).[28]

PROLOGUE 25–28

These people reverence God, and do not become elated
over their good deeds; they judge it is God's strength,
not their own, that brings about the good in them. "They
praise" (Ps. 15:4) the Holy One working in them, and say
with the prophet: "Not to us, O God, not to us give the
glory, but to your name alone" (Ps. 115:1).[29]

PROLOGUE 29–30

30 To drive home the point made in Prologue 29–30, Benedict notes that the apostle Paul acknowledged God's power in his life.

31 Benedict closes with an appeal to listen to Christ's words and take action, quoting from the Sermon on the Mount: build your house upon the rock of Christ.

〰 Benedict has completed the criteria for living in the kingdom of God. In the remaining verses of the Prologue he assures us of God's love and support, and urges us to act *now*. Not only does God have patience, God is also guiding us to clean up our act; to repent and turn back to God.

32 A delay or a period of grace.

〰 Although not in the Rule, the phrase "Always we begin again" has come to be identified with Benedictine living. Daily we begin again to live for Christ and by the Gospels. We listen for God's voice and respond with the action we discern that God is calling us to do. This is Benedictine obedience and the message of the Prologue.

In just this way Paul the apostle refused to take credit
for the power of his preaching. He declared: "By God's
grace I am what I am" (1 Cor. 15:10). And again Paul
said: "They who boast should make their boast in God"
(2 Cor. 10:17).[30] That is why it is said in the Gospel:
"Whoever hears these words of mine and does them is like
a wise person who built a house upon rock; the floods came
and the winds blew and beat against the house, but it did
not fall: it was founded on rock" (Matt. 7:24–25).[31]

PROLOGUE 31–34

With this conclusion, God waits for us daily to translate
into action, as we should, these holy teachings. Therefore
our life span has been lengthened by way of a truce,[32] that
we may amend our misdeeds. As the apostle says: "Do
you not know that the patience of God is leading you to
repent?" (Rom. 2:4). And indeed God assures us in love: "I
do not wish the death of sinners, but that they turn back to
me and live" (Ezek. 33:11).

PROLOGUE 35–38

~ In Prologue 39–44, Benedict again brings up the need for choice in two more "if" statements: if action is taken and if eternal life is desired. Three words describe what a monastic is to do: Prepare—Pray—Hurry. We can do the same.

33 Benedict calls once again for obedience. To this end, the whole person is to prepare—heart and body. This is a spiritual discipline; the monastic works to control bodily desires that can inhibit the journey to God. Obedience will be a battle, echoing Prologue 1.

34 Again countering the Pelagian view, Benedict reminds us to pray to God to provide what we lack.

35 The image of "light of life" echoes Prologue 13. Benedict continues with a sense of urgency. Think long term. Act now while there is still time. Run!

~ I understand eternal life but hell is another story. To me, Jesus offers us the way to living fully today. According to Cistercian monk Michael Casey, "Heaven is the state of being fully open to the more abundant life that Jesus came to offer us; hell is simply our freely decided refusal to take up that offer...." (Casey).

In spite of how I personally struggle with the idea of a hell, I must acknowledge its place in the Rule. Father Casey closes his reflection on eternal life and hell with these words:

> If we wish to arrive at unending life, now is the time to start choosing life in all we do. If we wish to flee the punishments of hell, now is the time to start avoiding self-destructive choices. The grace of God calls us to walk the road that leads to eternal life, but whether we choose to pursue this path, for all practical purposes, depends on us. Today I set before you life and death: choose life. (Casey)

May we all choose life.

Now that we have asked God who will dwell in the holy tent, we have heard the instruction for dwelling in it, but only if we fulfill the obligations of those who live there. We must, then, prepare our hearts and bodies for the battle of holy obedience to God's instructions.[33] What is not possible to us by nature, let us ask the Holy One to supply by the help of grace.[34] If we wish to reach eternal life, even as we avoid the torments of hell, then—while there is still time, while we are in this body and have time to accomplish all these things by the light of life—we must run and do now what will profit us forever.[35]

PROLOGUE 39–44

36 The Latin word *schola* can have different meanings: a place of service or practice, a group gathered for a common purpose, a time of preparation, or even instruction under a master (Kardong). In the Rule, "service" generally refers to "mutual service," the primary way that members serve God (Kardong).

37 Is Benedict following the words of Jesus, who promised an easy yoke and a light burden (Matthew 11:30)? Here we find Benedict's compassion for the members as well as his preference for moderation, which we will see throughout the Rule.

38 Limits and norms are needed to protect the community as a whole as well as the members.

⟿ What hopeful words! We do not have to hurry by ourselves. We can be part of Benedict's school as we learn about and take on some Benedictine practices. Oblates, church groups, Benedictine study groups all become part of Benedict's school.

39 Benedict offers an image for the journey. The unstated promise is that as the road is traveled, it will widen and the journey will become easier.

40 Monastic life—and Christian life—is a process to be lived in faithfulness. As we follow Christ, God's love will be poured into our hearts (Romans 5:5) and that love will be of such delight as to defy any description. This is not necessarily a love that brings an emotion within us. It is a love that seeks the best for another person and leads us to help make that happen.

Therefore we intend to establish a school for God's service.[36] In drawing up its regulations, we hope to set down nothing harsh, nothing burdensome.[37] The good of all concerned, however, may prompt us to a little strictness in order to amend faults and to safeguard love.[38]

PROLOGUE 45–47

Do not be daunted immediately by fear and run away from the road that leads to salvation. It is bound to be narrow at the outset.[39] But as we progress in this way of life and in faith, we shall run on the path of God's commandments, our hearts overflowing with the inexpressible delight of love.[40]

PROLOGUE 48–49

41 Benedict no longer speaks of making a choice as he had through much of the Prologue. He trusts that his monastics have made their choice and closes with a positive picture of this life embraced in faith. Patience will be shown as they grow in the monastic life, confronting not only their faults but also dealing in love with the challenges of living with others.

Prologue 45–50 offers an excellent example of Benedict's changes to the Rule of the Master (RM), an important resource used by Benedict. Prologue 45–47 and 50 were drawn from RM. Benedict added verses 48–49, most likely through the influence of the rules of Augustine. These verses reveal to me how much Benedict wanted his monastics to say Yes to God and to monastic life. And so he offers hope, encouragement, and assurance. As we continue to explore the Rule you will see other ways that this concern for the souls of his monastics is revealed.

Never swerving from God's instructions, then, but faithfully observing God's teaching in the monastery until death, we shall through patience share in the sufferings of Christ that we may deserve also to share in the eternal presence. Amen.[41]

PROLOGUE 50

The Divine Office

1 Meeting in community for prayer is the main work of the Benedictine monastic. The defining characteristic of the Benedictine monastery is the Divine Office, in Latin *Opus Dei* (the Work of God), the schedule of community prayer around which all other activities are organized.

Early monastic communities looked to Holy Scripture to direct their lives and worship. Scripture determined the frequency of the services, which began long before dawn and continued at intervals throughout the day. The services were chanted, using a form of singing in unison such as Gregorian chant. The Night Office, or Vigils, was sung in the middle of the night and Lauds, the first Office of the day, came before dawn. The next five services were roughly every three hours with Compline, the closing Office, said before bed. Work, personal prayer, meals, and rest were structured around these eight services. Appearing in written form in the fourth century, the Offices combine prayer, psalms and other scripture, and musical responses to scripture called canticles. Benedict meticulously explains the liturgy of the Divine Office in chapters 8 through 19 of the Rule.

Today some monasteries continue the tradition of eight services. Others meet two to four times a day for Morning Prayer (combining Vigils and Lauds), a noonday service, Vespers (Evening Prayer), and Compline, the closing Office. These services are also called the Daily Office. Stopping what they are doing and turning intentionally to God helps monastics find God outside the Divine Office so that all life becomes prayer. What would it be like to stop even for a moment at different times throughout the day and turn to God to say a prayer or give thanks?

2 □ Turning to God

The Divine Office and Prayer

What does Benedict say about prayer? Plenty! In this chapter we will look at how the monastery prays together, the role of prayer in work, and personal prayer. Benedict also provides instructions for how to create an environment that supports prayer and structures time for prayer.

The prophet says: "Seven times a day have I praised you" (Ps. 119: 164). We will fulfill this sacred number of seven if we satisfy our obligations of service at Lauds, Prime, Terce, Sext, None, Vespers and Compline, for it was of these hours during the day that it was said: "Seven times a day have I praised you" (Ps. 119:164). Concerning Vigils, the same prophet says: "At midnight I arose to give you praise" (Ps. 119:62).[1]

CHAPTER 16. THE CELEBRATION OF THE DIVINE OFFICE DURING THE DAY, 1–4

2 Ordinary days are those other than Sundays, feast days when saints and holy people are remembered, and days outside of the Advent–Christmas and Lent–Easter seasons. This description of Lauds illustrates the liturgy and Benedict's detailed instructions.

3 To be late to the Divine Office is disrespectful to the community and to God, and has consequences, as we will see shortly. So with a compassionate and understanding heart, Benedict provides a way to slide in under the wire.

4 Poetic scripture that is usually sung.

5 Literally in Greek, "a word of glory to God." These words would be different from the seventeenth-century doxology familiar to many of us: "Praise God from whom all blessings flow."

6 A reading from one of the letters of Paul from the New Testament. Although Benedict's monks could read, memorization was considered important, as it had been in earlier monasticism. Verses from the Bible would be recalled throughout the day.

7 A short text recited between one person and the congregation.

8 Ambrose (340–387 CE), recognized as one of the four great doctors of the Western Church, introduced congregational singing and wrote many hymns.

9 A verse coupled with a response by the congregation.

10 A form of prayer consisting of petitions and congregational responses.

11 The "Prayer of Jesus" is the Lord's Prayer. Benedict truly understands human nature and the tendency to hold tight to resentments and anger that can injure relationships and community. The Lord's Prayer is a reminder to both forgive and be forgiven.

On ordinary weekdays, Lauds are celebrated as follows.[2] First, Psalm 67 is said without a refrain and slightly protracted as on Sunday so that everyone can be present for Psalm 51, which has a refrain.[3] Next, according to custom, two more psalms are said in the following order: on Monday, Psalms 5 and 36; on Tuesday, Psalms 43 and 57; on Wednesday, Psalms 64–65; on Thursday, Psalms 88 and 90; on Friday, Psalms 76 and 92; on Saturday, Psalm 143 and the Canticle[4] from Deuteronomy, divided into two sections, with the Doxology[5] after each section. On other days, however, a Canticle from the prophets is said, according to the practice of the Roman Church. Next follow Psalms 148 through 150, a reading from the apostle recited by heart,[6] a responsory,[7] an Ambrosian hymn,[8] a versicle,[9] the Gospel canticle, the litany[10] and conclusion.

Assuredly, the celebration of Lauds and Vespers must never pass by without the prioress or abbot reciting the entire Prayer of Jesus at the end for all to hear, because thorns of contention are likely to spring up. Thus warned by the pledge they make to one another in the very words of this prayer: "Forgive us as we forgive" (Matt. 6:12), they may cleanse themselves of this kind of vice.[11]

CHAPTER 13. THE CELEBRATION OF LAUDS ON ORDINARY DAYS, 1–11, 12–13

12   Benedict shows concern for the monastics by suggesting a "reasonable" time to rise for Vigils. The eighth hour refers to the hours of the solar night, and not clock time. Benedict's monks probably retired about 7 p.m. and rose about 2 a.m. in winter (Kardong). There were no watches, clocks, or smartphones to alert them to the time. At night a device that dripped water (water clock) may have been used.

13   Another name for the book of Psalms.

14   Benedict believes that idleness is the enemy of the soul (RB 48.1) and so suggests here that time between Vigils and Lauds be used wisely for study. Monastics would study texts to prepare for the Divine Office. How do you and I use the time between our major activities of the day? Do we fill our minds with valuable and uplifting reading or do we opt for the smartphone and computer games?

15   Showing flexibility that considers the needs of the members, Benedict adjusts the time for Vigils in response to the changing length of the day and night.

~   Have you ever gotten up in the middle of the night to pray? I am in awe of this practice and, thus far, have experienced it only once while visiting Mount Saint Mary's Abbey in Wrentham, Massachusetts, a monastery of Cistercian nuns. There is something powerful and mystical about meeting in community for prayer at an hour when we are usually fast asleep. I recall, after the service, looking out my window onto the cloister where a nun sat quietly reading until sunrise and Lauds. There was a sense of total rightness and peace.

During the winter season, that is, from the first of November until Easter, it seems reasonable to arise at the eighth hour of the night.[12] By sleeping until a little past the middle of the night, the community can arise with their food fully digested. In the time remaining after Vigils, those who need to learn some of the psalter[13] or readings should study them.[14]

Between Easter and the first of November mentioned above, the time for Vigils should be adjusted so that a very short interval after Vigils will give the members opportunity to care for nature's needs. Then, at daybreak, Lauds should follow immediately.[15]

CHAPTER 8. THE DIVINE OFFICE AT NIGHT, 1–3, 4

16 After going into great detail about what psalms to use at each of the eight services, including variations for Sundays, Benedict not only opens the door to modify or change his suggestions but also actually *encourages* this with his opening words. But the invitation has a standard—use all 150 psalms.

17 Another translation reads "are sluggards in the performance of their devotion" (Kardong), clearly expressing Benedict's extreme distaste for the laziness in this important monastic occupation.

18 I deeply appreciate the way that Benedict is not stuck on his own ideas. He generously considers that there may be other ways to approach the Divine Office. His flexibility is found in many places in the Rule. Here he opens the door for us to pray the Divine Office in contemporary ways, such as using resources available online or through apps. Benedict includes himself in those he calls "lukewarm." I seriously doubt that he was but it is a lovely expression of humility by this gracious and caring abbot.

Above all else we urge that if people find this distribution of the psalms unsatisfactory, they should arrange whatever they judge better, provided that the full complement of one hundred and fifty psalms is by all means carefully maintained every week, and that the series begins anew each Sunday at Vigils.[16] For members who in a week's time say less than the full psalter with the customary canticles betray extreme indolence and lack of devotion in their service.[17] We read, after all, that our holy ancestors, energetic as they were, did all this in a single day. Let us hope that we, lukewarm as we are, can achieve it in a whole week.[18]

CHAPTER 18. THE ORDER OF PSALMODY, 22–25

19 Benedict gives instructions for conduct so that respect for others and the Divine Office is maintained. That he cautions against "frivolity" must mean than there *was* occasionally frivolity in the monastery.

I understand Benedict's concern about conduct prior to singing the Divine Office. In the choir we can spend time talking and guffawing right before we begin worship. As fifth-century monk and chronicler of Egyptian monasticism John Cassian cautions concerning prayer, we bring into the room what we were doing before we arrive. He directs us to put ourselves in the state of mind that we wish to have in prayer before we begin to pray (Cassian).

How many of us wait until the last minute to leave for an appointment, meeting, or worship service? I can do that and end up rushing about madly. Even at a monastery when the bell is rung ten minutes before the service calling all to prayer, I will keep doing things until the last minute. Instead of squeezing in one more thing, let's allow ourselves enough leeway to arrive on time and calmly.

20 Benedict reminds monastics of the priority of the Opus Dei, a priority that comes from the love of Christ.

On hearing the signal for an hour of the Divine Office, monastics will immediately set aside what they have in hand and go with utmost speed, yet with gravity and without giving occasion for frivolity.[19] Indeed, nothing is to be preferred to the Opus Dei.[20]

CHAPTER 43. TARDINESS AT THE OPUS DEI OR AT TABLE, 1–3

21 Given its central place in the life of the community and the importance of reverence to God, the Work of God (the Divine Office or Opus Dei) in the oratory (the chapel) calls for respectful and focused attention. To make satisfaction is to be repentant for what was done and willing to make amends to the community.

22 One aspect of humility is accepting ourselves as we are and being willing to admit when we are wrong.

23 Ouch! Benedict is really firm here, perhaps too firm for our taste, especially the instruction to whip children. It may seem to us that such strictness might create an environment of fear rather than of peace, as Benedict desires. In the sixth century, however, physical punishment was used more frequently than today.

~ In spite of how we may feel about Benedict's discipline, we can take something important from this chapter: our minds can wander and because of this we can make mistakes. Instead, we can strive to be fully present when we worship, when we pray, and when we are in conversation with each other, setting aside an imagined conversation or wandering thoughts.

Should monastics make a mistake in a psalm, responsory, refrain or reading, they must make satisfaction there before all.[21] If they do not use this occasion to humble themselves,[22] they will be subjected to more severe punishment for failing to correct by humility the wrong committed through negligence. Youth, however, are to be whipped for such a fault.[23]

CHAPTER 45. MISTAKES IN THE ORATORY, 1–3

24 In a key passage from the Rule, Benedict reminds us that God is everywhere and in every place. "We imagine the Divine as distant and inaccessible, whereas in fact we live steeped in its burning layers" (de Chardin). And so we can find the sacred in even the most ordinary things. That God's eyes are on us need not be taken fearfully but as assurance that God knows us and is ready to help us. With God everywhere there is no place or time that we cannot turn to God in prayer.

25 Benedict again reminds his community of the importance of the Divine Office.

26 Benedict uses Holy Scripture to emphasize the importance of attentiveness in the Divine Office. To have minds in harmony with voices is to be fully present to the moment. This instruction for mindfulness is a spiritual discipline found not only in Christianity but also in other religions.

≈ Chapter 19 is one of my favorite chapters in the Rule. Because God is everywhere, everything is sacred, from the most beautiful stained glass window to the rocks that litter my garden. Every moment is sacred, too, permeated with the presence of God. Benedict reminds us to always be in the present moment, so that our eyes, ears, minds, and hearts are open to God. Wherever we are and whatever we are doing at that moment, let's strive to bring our full attention to the person or task at hand and find God in our midst.

27 This is one of the few places that Benedict mentions the Trinity, perhaps including it to show that his monastery follows the orthodox view that accepted the doctrine of the Trinity. Not all Christians believed in the Trinity in Benedict's time, such as the Arians who believed that Jesus Christ was created by God and was therefore unequal to God the Father.

28 Here Benedict makes another reference to following the orthodoxy of the early Church.

We believe that the divine presence is everywhere and "that in every place the eyes of God are watching the good and the wicked" (Prov. 15:3).[24] But beyond the least doubt we should believe this to be especially true when we celebrate the Divine Office.[25]

We must always remember, therefore, what the prophet says: "Serve the Holy One with reverence" (Ps. 2:11), and again, "Sing praise wisely" (Ps. 47:8); and, "in the presence of the angels I will sing to you" (Ps. 138:1). Let us consider, then, how we ought to behave in the presence of God and God's angels, and let us stand to sing the psalms in such a way that our minds are in harmony with our voices.[26]

CHAPTER 19. THE DISCIPLINE OF PSALMODY, 1–2, 3–7

As soon as the cantor begins to sing the Doxology, let all rise from their seats in honor and reverence for the Holy Trinity.[27] Besides the inspired books of the Old and New Testaments, the works read at Vigils should include explanations of Scripture by reputable and orthodox writers.[28]

CHAPTER 9. THE NUMBER OF PSALMS AT THE NIGHT OFFICE, 7–8

29 The Gospels are given special honor because they contain the story of Jesus.

30 Whenever Benedict uses "God forbid" we know that he is relating an *extremely* serious occurrence that he hopes *never* happens. I will point out other occurrences as we go along.

31 Because of the importance of the psalms, Benedict shortens other scripture and responses.

32 Monastics may work in the fields or away from the monastery. Wherever they are, the Divine Office is an obligation, priority, and joy, and so must be honored.

While there is a need to be flexible, I find that I become lax in my prayer time when I am away from home. Benedict reminds me not to use travel as an excuse to neglect my time with God, but to do my best to continue to set aside time for prayer, even if that time is shortened.

A closing thought on the Divine Office from a contemporary Cistercian monk:

> To love Christ is to love prayer, to be ready at every moment to drop everything and hurry to that place where God is about to speak his word to us and is waiting for our response … nothing is more important than the one work for which the monk has come to the monastery—the work of God. (Louf)

When that is finished, they read from the Gospels while all stand with respect and awe.²⁹

This arrangement for Sunday Vigils should be followed at all times, summer and winter, unless— God forbid—the members happen to arise too late.³⁰ In that case, the readings or responsories will have to be shortened.³¹ Let special care be taken that this not happen, but if it does, the one at fault is to make due satisfaction to God in the oratory.

CHAPTER 11. THE CELEBRATION OF VIGILS ON SUNDAY, 9, 11–13

Members who work so far away that they cannot return to the oratory at the proper time—and the prioress or abbot determines that is the case—are to perform the Opus Dei where they are, and kneel out of reverence for God.³²

So too, those who have been sent on a journey are not to omit the prescribed hours but to observe them as best they can, not neglecting their measure of service.

CHAPTER 50. MEMBERS WORKING AT A DISTANCE OR TRAVELING, 1–4

Personal Prayer

33 In chapter 4 Benedict outlines "the tools for the spiritual craft" (4.75) and instructs monastics to devote themselves often to prayer. Holy reading, *lectio divina* in Latin, is a slow, prayerful reading of Holy Scripture or other spiritual texts where the person praying listens for God's voice to speak through the words. This way of prayer, first practiced by the Desert Fathers and Mothers, is a way to listen with the ear of the heart (Prologue 1).

34 Prayer with tears was thought to be the deepest and most profound prayer, coming when the monastic had a heartfelt understanding of his or her sinful nature. Such prayer was a prelude to change. Amending our ways is still an important practice for spiritual growth and the quest for eternal life.

Lectio divina has been the mainstay of my prayer for twenty-five years. When a word or phrase catches my attention, my slow reading stops and I reflect on the connection of the word or phrase to my life. Conversation with God (prayer) about these connections follows. There are times when nothing catches my attention, but there are many times when I hear God through the words of scripture, guiding me or giving me hope, pointing out wrong opinions or uncharitable actions. I can then change my ways, as Benedict asks.

Listen readily to holy reading, and devote yourself often to prayer.[33] Every day with tears and sighs confess your past sins to God in prayer and change from these evil ways in the future.[34]

CHAPTER 4. THE TOOLS FOR GOOD WORKS, 55–58

35 From the time of the Desert Fathers and Mothers, idleness was seen as an opportunity for the devil to sabotage a monastic's relationship with God. Benedict inherited this tradition and so arranges specific time periods for work and *lectio divina*.

36 *Lectio divina* is so important to the spiritual health and progress of each individual that Benedict sends senior monastics to help members concentrate on their reading.

37 Another "God forbid." For Benedict it is unthinkable that monastics should neglect their reading or distract others from their reading. The reason is not to keep a rule but to preserve the souls of the members in their search for God.

38 This seems to imply that in Benedict's monastery there were appropriate times for members to simply hang out with each other. And there still are today.

I will admit that there are times that I go looking for distractions when I am doing *lectio divina*. Perhaps my prayer that day is boring or I do not feel that I am getting anywhere. Maybe the phone rings and instead of continuing my conversation with God, I spring up from my chair and flee to the kitchen to partake of something I deem, at that moment, more pleasant. God forbid!

Idleness is the enemy of the soul. Therefore, the community members should have specified periods for manual labor as well as for prayerful reading.[35]

Above all, one or two elders must surely be deputed to make the rounds of the monastery while the members are reading.[36] Their duty is to see that no one is so apathetic as to waste time or engage in idle talk to the neglect of their reading, and so not only harm themselves but also distract others. If such persons are found—God forbid—they should be reproved a first and a second time.[37] If they do not amend, they must be subjected to the punishment of the rule as a warning to others. Further, members ought not to associate with one another at inappropriate times.[38]

CHAPTER 48. THE DAILY MANUAL LABOR, 1, 17–21

39 Benedict asks for both devotion and humility, recognizing that God is to be completely reverenced.

40 Purity of heart was an objective of monastic life that came out of the early monastic movement. "To strive for purity of heart is to strive for a life totally given to God, following Christ in both thought and action" (Tomaine).

41 "Compunction" means "to jab" or "to prick severely." In other words, the recognition of sins and mistakes is to jab monastics in the heart so that changed actions follow. It is not many words that count, Benedict says, but an intense feeling of regret in the recognition of our sins.

42 Benedict seems to understand that minds can wander. Therefore, prayer is to be kept short unless under divine inspiration.

43 Time for silent prayer in the Divine Office is always short so that the flow of the service is not interrupted.

Whenever we want to ask a favor of someone powerful, we do it humbly and respectfully, for fear of presumption. How much more important, then, to lay our petitions before the God of all with the utmost humility and sincere devotion.[39] We must know that God regards our purity of heart[40] and tears of compunction, not our many words.[41] Prayer should therefore be short and pure, unless perhaps it is prolonged under the inspiration of divine grace.[42] In community, however, prayer should always be brief; and when the prioress or abbot gives the signal, all should rise together.[43]

CHAPTER 20. REVERENCE IN PRAYER, 1–5

44 Prayer is woven into the fabric of monastic work. In the Prologue, Benedict instructs monastics to pray to God before beginning a task (Prologue 4). Prayers are also offered by and for members beginning and completing kitchen service and reading at meals. These prayers take place in the oratory, reinforcing the presence of God and the sacredness of this service to others. In the Rule kitchen service is closely bound together with religion and symbolizes following Jesus, who served at table and gave his life for the human community (Kardong). The abbot or prioress blesses members entering and leaving kitchen service. The giving of blessings appears throughout the Rule and must help monastics remember the presence of God in their work and among each other.

45 John Cassian named this scripture the one prayer "absolutely necessary for possessing the perpetual awareness of God" (Cassian). This psalm verse appears in the Divine Office beginning with Prime around 6 a.m. and in each service that follows, including Compline in the evening. The verse is an important reminder to continually turn to God.

~ Given the scripture chosen to end and begin kitchen service (Psalm 86:17 and 70:2), I get the sense that this job was a challenging one so prayers were needed. I love the way Benedict frames work with prayer. What if we look at our work in the kitchen as sacred service and ask for God's help as we begin and give thanks for God's help when we finish?

On Sunday immediately after Lauds, those beginning
as well as those completing their week of service should
make a profound bow in the oratory before all and ask for
their prayers. Let the server completing the week recite
this verse: "Blessed are you, O God, who have helped me
and comforted me" (Dan. 3:52, Ps. 86:17). After this verse
has been said three times the server receives a blessing.[44]
Then the one beginning the service follows and says: "O
God, come to my assistance; O God, make haste to help
me" (Ps. 70:2).[45] And all repeat this verse three times.
When they have received a blessing, the servers begin
their service.

CHAPTER 35. KITCHEN SERVERS OF THE WEEK, 15–18

46 Benedict structures monastic life to create an organized, harmonious, and peaceful environment.

47 Vanity was one of the eight troublesome thoughts written about by the fourth-century Christian monk and ascetic Evagrius Ponticus. Other thoughts named that would interfere with spiritual progress were gluttony, lust, greed, anger, sadness, pride, and *acedia* (weariness of soul or disdain). Later, *acedia* was dropped and the list became known as the Seven Deadly Sins.

48 This verse also opens Lauds; a prayer that God be present in all that is spoken.

[∿] I love to read scripture alone and in worship. Because I think that I do a pretty good job at this, perhaps I also need the prayers of the community to shield *me* from vanity!

Praying for Others

49 Benedict asks his members to pray for others, here following Jesus's instructions in the Sermon on the Mount (Matthew 5:44). Our own love of Christ can help us offer this often difficult prayer.

50 "Excommunication" means exclusion from the community for meals, prayer, and working with others. Discipline in the Rule gives monastics opportunities to amend behavior. The bottom line is that love should dominate and prayer is in order.

51 Blessings are important in the Rule. Blessings are asked from a visitor (RB 53.24, 66.3), given after penance (RB 44.10), and withheld for serious faults (RB 25.6). Although primarily given by the abbot or prioress, monastics can also give, withhold, or ask for blessings.

Reading will always accompany the meals. The reader should not be the one who just happens to pick up the book, but someone who will read for a whole week, beginning on Sunday.[46] After Mass and Communion, let the incoming reader ask all to pray so that God may shield them from the spirit of vanity.[47] Let the reader begin this verse in the oratory: "O God, open my lips, and my mouth shall proclaim your praise" (Ps. 51:17), and let all say it three times.[48] When they have received a blessing, they will begin their week of reading.

CHAPTER 38. THE READER FOR THE WEEK, 1–4

Pray for your enemies out of love for Christ.[49]

CHAPTER 4. THE TOOLS FOR GOOD WORKS, 72

Rather, as the apostle also says: "Let love be reaffirmed" (2 Cor. 2:8), and let all pray for the one who is excommunicated.[50]

CHAPTER 27. THE CONCERN OF THE ABBOT AND PRIORESS
FOR THE EXCOMMUNICATED, 4

Wherever members meet, the junior asks the elder for a blessing. [51]

CHAPTER 63. COMMUNITY RANK, 15

52 Contact with the world outside the monastery presented possible temptations, sights, and sounds that could draw members from their path to God and their fidelity to monastic life and the Rule. Therefore, the community would pray for members before departure, at each service of the Divine Office, and upon their return. Monastic communities today pray for absent members.

When I was in high school I had a friend whose mother would bid us farewell with these words: "I'll pray for you." I thought it a bit odd at the time but see now how it covered Katie and me with a special protective blessing.

The temptations, sights, and sounds that can draw twenty-first-century people away from their path to God are often related to technology. Minutes and hours can be frittered away on trivia. Do I *really* need to check the weather forecast every hour and cast an eye on my email as soon as the alarm goes off in the morning?

53 When received as a member of the monastic community, the novice writes out a document promising faithfulness to monastic life, the community, the abbot or prioress, and the Rule. After the document is placed on the altar, the novice asks for God's help. The community repeats the verse, which gives all an opportunity to recall their own vows. That the novice would prostrate (lie flat on the floor on his or her stomach) at the feet of each member individually is a powerful expression of connectedness of members within the community. His or her growth in monastic life will be influenced by others—their support, their prayers, their understanding. As we work together with others and even in our families, perhaps we can prostrate in our hearts before them in a silent prayer for connection, support, and understanding.

Members sent on a journey will ask the prioress or abbot and the community to pray for them. All absent members should always be remembered at the closing prayer of the Opus Dei. When they come back from a journey, they should, on the very day of their return, lie face down on the floor of the oratory at the conclusion of each of the customary hours of the Opus Dei. They ask the prayers of all for their faults, in case they may have been caught off guard on the way by seeing some evil thing or hearing some idle talk.[52]

CHAPTER 67. MEMBERS SENT ON A JOURNEY, 1–4

... the novice begins the verse: "Receive me, O God, as you have promised, and I shall live; do not disappoint me in my hope" (Ps. 119:116). The whole community repeats the verse three times, and adds the Doxology. Then the novices prostrate themselves at the feet of each member to ask prayers, and from that very day they are to be counted as one of the community.[53]

CHAPTER 58. THE PROCEDURE FOR RECEIVING MEMBERS, 21–23

Times for Prayer

In addition to the Divine Office and other corporate and personal prayers discussed above, Benedict instructs his community to share prayer with others, such as before and after meals (RB 43.13, 17), or pray privately at different times.

54 Hospitality to guests is an important spiritual practice in the Rule. Once the guest is greeted, prayer follows. Scholars are not exactly sure what Benedict means by first sharing prayer before the kiss of peace. The prayer could have been a kind of litmus test to identify those who followed the current orthodoxy of the Church and with whom the kiss of peace could be exchanged (Kardong). Benedict may have been on the lookout for Arian Christians (see note 27 above). Prayer also shows the guest that the community is centered in God.

Praying when we meet new people is a way that we can put our interactions with them into a holy space. What if we said a silent prayer whenever we met a new person?

55 Benedict provides plenty of time for the important work of holy reading (*lectio divina*). He increases the time for *lectio divina* during Lent.

When we are not part of a community with allotted times for prayer, it is difficult to maintain a discipline of prayer in regular intervals throughout the day. One reason people outside monastic community write and follow a rule of life for themselves is to have a daily structure to ensure time with God in prayer.

First of all, [the community and guests] are to pray together and thus be united in peace, but prayer must always precede the kiss of peace[54] because of the delusions of the devil.

CHAPTER 53. THE RECEPTION OF GUESTS, 4–5

From the first of October to the beginning of Lent, the members ought to devote themselves to reading until the end of the second hour…. Then after their meal they will devote themselves to their reading or to the psalms.[55]

CHAPTER 48. THE DAILY MANUAL LABOR, 10, 13

Creating an Environment to Support Prayer

56 Silence has always been a part of monastic rules because silence helps the monk or nun listen for the promptings of God without disturbance. Benedict knows that being silent is not easy; it must be cultivated.

57 The rule of silence is so important in Benedict's community that breaking this rule has serious consequences. Benedict does not always give us specifics of what the punishments might be. We will be looking at discipline in other chapters of this book. Notice that the rule of silence may be broken in order to meet the needs of a guest or the community. Flexibility such as this is characteristic of the Rule of Benedict.

◇ Monasteries I have visited all have silence after Compline or after a certain hour. In our busy and talkative world, experiencing silence is restorative and profound. Usually guest rooms have thin walls so it is with gratitude that most of us greet the "Great Silence" of the overnight hours, when we can silently pray, read, or rest. Snoring can be an issue, however. Benedict says nothing about this.

Monastics should diligently cultivate silence at all times,
but especially at night.

When all have assembled, they should pray Compline;
and on leaving Compline, no one will be permitted to
speak further.[56] If monastics are found to transgress this rule
of silence, they must be subjected to severe punishment,
except on occasions when guests require attention or the
prioress or abbot wishes to give someone a command, but
even this is to be done with the utmost seriousness and
proper restraint.[57]

CHAPTER 42. SILENCE AFTER COMPLINE, 1, 8–11

～ Each verse in chapter 52 cautions monastics against actions that would disturb other members and show a lack of respect.

58 The chapel is for prayer and nothing else. Storage of stuff is a distraction and shows a lack of honor for the true function of the space—the worship of God.

59 It sounds like Benedict had dealt with monastics who were thoughtless and disrespectful of others.

60 Benedict's favorite and most meaningful type of prayer is one of tears and love.

～ Anyone who has attended a religious service has probably experienced the cacophony that follows the closing words, where the din of voices competes with the organ postlude. Forgetting that we were there to praise God, we move quickly into personal chatting. Benedict will have none of this—someone may have been especially moved by the service or may have a personal concern and therefore may want to stay and pray privately. This must be respected.

61 In Benedict's day personal reading was generally not done silently but spoken or whispered.

～ As we close this chapter, I offer a prayer that has been associated with Benedict.

> Gracious and holy Father, give us wisdom to perceive you, intelligence to understand you, diligence to seek you, patience to wait for you, eyes to behold you, a heart to meditate on you, and a life to proclaim you; through the power of the Spirit of Jesus Christ our Lord. Amen (Counsell).

The oratory ought to be what it is called, and nothing else is to be done or stored there.[58] After the Opus Dei, all should leave in complete silence and with reverence for God, so that anyone who may wish to pray alone will not be disturbed by the insensitivity of another.[59] Moreover, if at other times some choose to pray privately, they may simply go in and pray, not in a loud voice, but with tears and heartfelt devotion.[60] Accordingly, those who do not pray in this manner are not to remain in the oratory after the Opus Dei, as we have said; then they will not interfere with anyone else.

CHAPTER 52. THE ORATORY OF THE MONASTERY, 1–5

But after Sext and their meal, they may rest on their beds in complete silence; should any members wish to read privately, let them do so, but without disturbing the others.[61]

CHAPTER 48. THE DAILY MANUAL LABOR, 5

The Kinds of Monastics

1 The first chapter in the Rule describes the four kinds of monastics first found in Christian monasticism of Egypt—cenobites, anchorites, sarabaites, and gyrovagues.

2 Benedict lists the characteristics of the cenobite, the monastic he favors, giving us two of the three vows or promises made by men and women entering a Benedictine community. First, belonging to a monastery means that cenobites promise faithfulness to the place and the people there. This is the essence of the vow of *stability*. Second, cenobites turn their lives over to the community, the Rule, and the abbot or prioress, and promise to follow the guidance and direction from each as God's voice. This describes the essence of the promise of *obedience*.

〰 Fleeing from people, places, or situations is contrary to the Benedictine vows, but fleeing is what we tend to do when encountering words like "stability" and "obedience." We do not want to be tied down, preferring to keep all options open, especially when situations get tense. But always being on the move in our personal and spiritual lives can create a sense of restlessness. Where do we settle in to uncover the richness of place, people, and pattern for our lives? Put down roots, Benedict says, and there you will find what you are looking for; there you will find God.

3 □ Seeking God

Monastic Identity and Vows

How does the Rule describe a Benedictine monk or nun, brother or sister? What is the process to enter a monastery and what promises are made? We will address these questions in this chapter. While Benedict was writing for the monks in his community, I am convinced that much of what he says can apply to us as well.

There are clearly four kinds of monastics.[1] First, there are the cenobites, that is to say, those who belong to a monastery, where they serve under a rule and an abbot or prioress.[2]

CHAPTER 1. THE KINDS OF MONASTICS, 1–2

3 While there were women and men in the early days of monasticism who went directly to the desert to live alone, Benedict feels that monastics must first live in the monastery, where they learn about themselves by living with others. Benedict's reference to "fervor of monastic life" introduces the third vow or promise taken by Benedictines—*conversion of life*; in Latin, *conversatio*. This vow is a single-minded and joyful commitment to the monastic way of life as outlined in the Rule. It means also being open to change and transformation in the process. Benedict's military imagery, commonly used in the early Church and in monastic writing, emphasizes the magnitude of the struggle to follow and be obedient to Christ.

〜 I appreciate Benedict's description of living in community as a test. What would it be like to spend month after month, 24/7, with people at work, people in our faith community, and those we see socially? Life in our communities is similar to life in a monastery. It takes a promise of stability—remaining connected to people and place—to stay there and learn. For those of us outside a monastery, *conversatio* means living fervently as a Christian, being open to transformation in that process.

Second, there are the anchorites or hermits, who have come through the test of living in a monastery for a long time, and have passed beyond the first fervor of monastic life. Thanks to the help and guidance of many, they are now trained to fight against evil. They have built up their strength and go from the battle line in the ranks of their members to the single combat of the desert.[3] Self-reliant now, without the support of another, they are ready with God's help to grapple single-handed with the vices of body and mind.

CHAPTER 1. THE KINDS OF MONASTICS, 3–5

4 "Sarabaite" in Coptic, the language of early monastic Egypt, means "separated from monasteries" (de Vogüé). The rule referred to here can mean either a written rule or a disciplined life, not necessarily Benedict's Rule (Böckmann).

5 Sarabaites are deceivers. Their words, actions, and even dress give the appearance of fidelity to the monastic life. But it is all a sham, Benedict says, because sarabaites follow their own desires.

6 No vow of obedience for sarabaites. They are prey to being misguided by their own willful decisions and actions, a way that makes them slaves to the whim and desire of the moment.

~ Now things are starting to hit closer to home. While I do not want to go off and live alone like a hermit, I like to do what I want and have been known to bend the rules to my liking. What if this rule bending hurts my relationship with God or with others? Will I even recognize this? We are not always the best judge of what to do. If we always live by our own whims we will not be challenged to grow. We need benchmarks that have been tried and proven to move us beyond the limited direction of self. This is what Benedict offers his community.

Third, there are sarabaites, the most detestable kind of monastics, who with no experience to guide them, no rule to try them as "gold is tried in a furnace" (Prov. 27:21), have a character as soft as lead.[4] Still loyal to the world by their actions, they clearly lie to God by their signs of religion.[5] Two or three together, or even alone, without a shepherd, they pen themselves up in their own sheepfolds, not God's. Their law is what they like to do, whatever strikes their fancy. Anything they believe in and choose, they call holy; anything they dislike, they consider forbidden.[6]

CHAPTER 1. THE KINDS OF MONASTICS, 6–9

7 "Gyrovague" is a word created by the abbot who wrote the Rule of the Master. To illustrate the characteristics of these monastics, he combined Greek *giro* (circle) and Latin *vagari* (wander, unstable) (Kardong).

8 Gyrovagues visit an anchorite or monastery where hospitality is an obligation and stay until they are asked to help out. Then they beat a hasty retreat and wander off to another monastery where they indulge their appetites and once more abuse hospitality. Stability to place and people? No way. Obedience to superiors and a rule? Too difficult.

∾ Have you ever encountered people who move from one church to another or who come into a community only to leave for one reason or another? Have you and I ever done that? Probably. Benedict cautions us against being wanderers. We can be slaves to ourselves, imprisoned in our own selfishness, or we can be slaves to Christ, and find freedom (1 Corinthians 7:22).

9 As Benedict embarks on writing the Rule for his community, he follows his own advice: pray before doing a good work. See "Opening Our Eyes to the Light from God," Prologue 4 and note 8.

10 Cenobites need to be strong because living full time in a monastic community is difficult. The days are long, the work repetitive, and the people sometimes frustrating. But in community, members can experience the personal and spiritual growth that will lead them to God and salvation. This is what Benedict wants for his monks and he knows all is possible through Christ.

∾ Perhaps we can pass on being a hermit, sarabaite, or gyrovague in our daily lives and instead do our best to follow Benedict's cenobites. Like the cenobites, we can be faithful to Christ, our relationships, and our communities. We can listen and respond to what we believe God is asking of us through people and situations. Finally, we can live fervently as Christians just like the cenobites who live fervently as monks or nuns.

Fourth and finally, there are the monastics called gyrovagues,[7] who spend their entire lives drifting from region to region, staying as guests for three or four days in different monasteries. Always on the move, they never settle down, and are slaves to their own wills and gross appetites. In every way they are worse than sarabaites.[8]

CHAPTER 1. THE KINDS OF MONASTICS, 10–11

It is better to keep silent than to speak of all these and their disgraceful way of life. Let us pass them by, then, and with the help of God,[9] proceed to draw up a plan for the strong kind, the cenobites.[10]

CHAPTER 1. THE KINDS OF MONASTICS, 12–13

The Vow of Stability

11 Throughout the Rule and here in chapter 4, Benedict guides the community toward stability. Remaining physically and emotionally connected to people and place is the exterior dimension of the vow. The inner dimension is an interior resting in God, an inner rootedness that gives strength and perseverance.

12 Benedict makes sure that the monastery itself supports the practice of stability and virtue, the latter also an important monastic goal. I love the use of "roam." Like the monks and nuns, we can lose our connection with what is truly important to us if we roam about all the distractions that can entice us every day.

13 Watchfulness is important in exercising both stability and obedience. Thoughts, actions, and words draw a monastic away from faithfulness and listening. Knowing that God observes everything can initially deter a new monastic from actions that undermine stability and obedience. But as an individual grows in the monastic life, love for God will supplant any fear and motivate the monastic to live in steadfastness and obedience.

∿ Remaining connected to people we would like to avoid mentally or physically is not easy, and being faithful takes persistence. Our thoughts, actions, and words can build walls between ourselves and others. Being aware of what we are thinking, doing, or saying will help us detect when we are about to put more brick into those walls.

14 Benedict often uses words like "always" and "constantly" as reminders for steadfastness, here to be faithful to the pursuit of purity of heart and virtue.

The workshop where we are to toil faithfully at all these tasks is the enclosure of the monastery and stability in the community.[11]

CHAPTER 4. THE TOOLS FOR GOOD WORKS, 78

The monastery should, if possible, be so constructed that within it all necessities, such as water, mill and garden are contained, and the various crafts are practiced. Then there will be no need for the members to roam outside, because this is not at all good for their souls.[12]

CHAPTER 66. THE PORTER OF THE MONASTERY, 6–7

While we guard ourselves at every moment from sins and vices of thought or tongue, of hand or foot, of self-will or bodily desire, let us recall that we are always seen by God in the heavens, that our actions everywhere are in God's sight and are reported by angels at every hour.[13]

CHAPTER 7. HUMILITY, 12–13

That we may take care to avoid sinful thoughts, we must always[14] say to ourselves: "I shall be blameless in God's sight if I guard myself from my own wickedness" (Ps. 18:24).

CHAPTER 7. HUMILITY, 18

15 Before accepting a visiting monastic permanently, Benedict wants to make sure that the person is not running away from another monastery (lack of stability) and that the abbot or prioress is not "stealing" a monastic from another community.

16 Benedict appears not too keen on letting priests into the monastery, most likely because he is concerned that it will be difficult for them to observe stability and obedience. Priests may be used to directing others rather than having others direct them. The monastic movement was originally a lay movement, so being prideful because of one's ordination may also have been a concern. Benedict's caution was not ultimately heeded. By the eighth century almost every monk was being ordained a priest (Kardong). Today women monastics can also be priests in denominations where women are ordained, such as the Episcopal Church. Monasteries continue to have members who are not ordained.

17 A cleric—a lower rank than bishop, priest, and deacon—must also promise obedience and stability.

~ As a priest myself, I am reminded by this chapter to not expect special favors because of my ordination. Benedict's concern has caused me never to wear a clerical collar when I lead retreats!

If after a while they wish to remain and bind themselves to stability, they should not be refused this wish, especially as there was time enough, while they were a guest, to judge their character.

The prioress and abbot must, however, take care never to receive into the community anyone from another known monastery, unless the prioress or abbot of that community consents and sends a letter or recommendation, since it is written: "Never do to another what you do not want done to yourself" (Tobit 4:16).[15]

CHAPTER 61. THE RECEPTION OF VISITING MONASTICS, 5, 13–14

If any ordained priest asks to be received into a male monastery, do not agree too quickly. However, if he is fully persistent in his request, he must recognize that he will have to observe the full discipline of the rule without any mitigation, knowing that it is written: "Friend, what have you come for?" (Matt. 26:50).[16]

Any clerics who similarly wish to join the community should be ranked somewhere in the middle, but only if they, too, promise to keep the rule and observe stability.[17]

CHAPTER 60. THE ADMISSION OF PRIESTS TO THE MONASTERY, 1–3, 8–9

18 While we may be shocked by this practice, in Benedict's day parents would bring children to the monastery, entering them into a lifelong commitment of stability with no say by the children. Benedict wants to remove the temptation of extra resources that could draw them away from steadfastness to the community and the Rule. The "God forbid" shows Benedict's horror and fear of losing a soul in this way.

The Vow of Obedience

19 The Latin word for "obedience" is *obaudire,* which means "to listen thoroughly." This means to listen "not just with the mind in an intellectual exercise, but with the heart, which is the root of love" and follow the instructions "willingly with the utmost energy and determination (Prologue 1)" (Tomaine). Obedience is to be immediate. Holy Scripture is the authority for obedience—the prioress and abbot are the presence of Christ in the monastery and so obedience to them is obedience to God. Monastics listen; then they respond to how God is calling them through the prioress or abbot, the Rule, and the community, as well as through scripture.

Benedict places the entire Rule in the realm of the spiritual—every action, word, and thought impacts the soul. Fear of hell and desire for everlasting life may initially motivate obedience. As the monk or nun grows in the monastic way of life, the love of Christ ultimately makes obedience easy and natural. Benedict devotes two chapters solely to the practice of obedience—chapter 5, which we will discuss next, and chapter 71, covered in this book's chapter 4, "Cultivating Love."

Many of us may think that obedience is what others owe *us*. But Benedictine obedience is about listening for the way God is calling us to take action to serve others, which may mean simply being a quiet presence for another person or even for ourselves. To listen we need to be in the present moment in order to discover how God is calling us. The next step is to follow that call. Therefore, obedience is listening and responding to God.

As to their property, they either make a sworn promise
in this document that they will never personally, never
through an intermediary, nor in any way at all, nor at
any time, give the child anything or afford the child the
opportunity to possess anything. This ought to leave no
way open for the child to entertain any expectations that
could deceive and lead to ruin. May God forbid this, but we
have learned from experience that it can happen.[18]

CHAPTER 59. THE OFFERING OF CHILDREN BY NOBLES OR THE POOR, 3, 6

The first step of humility is unhesitating obedience, which
comes naturally to those who cherish Christ above all.
Because of the holy service they have professed, or because
of dread of hell and for the glory of everlasting life, they
carry out the orders of the prioress or abbot as promptly as
if the command came directly from God. The Holy One
says of people like this: "No sooner did they hear than
they obeyed me" (Ps. 18:45); again, God tells teachers:
"Whoever listens to you, listens to me" (Luke 10:16).[19]

CHAPTER 5. OBEDIENCE, 1–6

20 A goal of monastic life is to replace self-will with God's will. Benedict asks us to abandon our own will. This can be perplexing. Doesn't God give us will and want us to exercise it? Perhaps our own will is focused more on self—on our own wants, desires, and plans—rather than on being present with an open heart to others.

21 Work is to be set aside to follow the new direction. The response of obedience is to be swift because of the love a monastic has for God. But are you like me and hate to leave anything unfinished? When a child is in need of care or a co-worker or friend is in need of a listening ear, the Rule asks us to *immediately* offer ourselves to the person or situation for our love of Christ. Obedience is part of all our relationships and a gift we can give to another.

22 Verses 10 and 11, found at the center of the chapter on obedience, express a central aspect of monastic life: the motivation for seeking eternal life is love—love of God and love of Christ—even though the road is narrow and challenging.

23 Benedict begins the last half of chapter 5 in verses 12–13 by returning to a description of abandoning self-will, which is choosing the cenobitic life. What makes obedience possible and positive for the monastic is that the abbot and prioress as well as all members of the community are committed to each other (stability) and have love at the root of all their actions (obedience).

〰 We also need community to support our efforts to turn from whim and appetite and follow Christ. We need community to challenge us when we miss that mark. Good friends, trusted family, a church group can become our "monastic" community of support as we seek God and God's plan for us.

Such people as these immediately put aside their own concerns, abandon their own will,[20] and lay down whatever they have in hand, leaving it unfinished. With the ready step of obedience, they follow the voice of authority in their actions. Almost at the same moment, then, as the teacher gives the instruction the disciple quickly puts it into practice out of reverence for God; and both actions together are swiftly completed as one.[21]

CHAPTER 5. OBEDIENCE, 7–9

It is love that impels them to pursue everlasting life; therefore, they are eager to take the narrow road of which God says: "Narrow is the road that leads to life" (Matt. 7:14).[22]

CHAPTER 5. OBEDIENCE, 10–11

They no longer live by their own judgment, giving in to their whims and appetites; rather they walk according to another's decisions and directions, choosing to live in monasteries and to have a prioress or abbot over them. Monastics of this resolve unquestionably conform to the saying of Christ: "I have come not to do my own will, but the will of the One who sent me" (John 6:38).[23]

CHAPTER 5. OBEDIENCE, 12–13

24 As he draws chapter 5 to a close, Benedict returns to the need for obedience to be swift, total, given freely, and offered gladly. Benedict cautions against the evil of grumbling, a subject that comes up frequently in the Rule. Grumbling is mentioned four times in chapter 5 alone.

25 By using Jesus's words from the Gospel of Luke, Benedict reinforces that the superior represents the voice of Christ in the community.

Do you ever grumble while you are doing a task? I certainly do and have even grumbled on occasion while writing this book! We could instead consider our tasks, especially the odious ones, as given to us by God to offer to God in service of others.

26 Here Benedict expands on the theme of grumbling to include grumbling both out loud and in one's heart. Murmuring is a serious matter because it threatens the harmony of the community and the spiritual health of the grumbler. In chapter 23 of the Rule, "Excommunication for Faults," punishment for grumbling progresses through two warnings, public admonishment, excommunication, and, finally, physical punishment should the grumbler not repent. Most of us recoil at the idea of physical punishment but it was part of the culture in Benedict's day.

Given the state of the world today, I like to believe that God will accept *any* good action, even if it is done with grumbling. Yet when I grumble in doing a task, my heart is far from God, which is the real danger for my soul.

This very obedience, however, will be acceptable to God and agreeable to people only if compliance with what is commanded is not cringing or sluggish or half-hearted, but free from any grumbling or any reaction of unwillingness.[24] For the obedience shown to an abbot or prioress is given to God, who has said: "Whoever listens to you, listens to me" (Luke 10:16).[25]

CHAPTER 5. OBEDIENCE, 14–15

Furthermore, the disciples' obedience must be given gladly, for "God loves a cheerful giver" (2 Cor. 9:7). If disciples obey grudgingly and grumble, not only aloud but also in their hearts, then, even though the order is carried out, their actions will not be accepted with favor by God, who sees that they are grumbling in their hearts. These disciples will have no reward for service of this kind; on the contrary, they will incur punishment for grumbling, unless they change for the better and make amends.[26]

CHAPTER 5. OBEDIENCE, 16–19

~ Benedict addresses obedience in other chapters of the Rule. We will first look at chapter 3 of the Rule, "Summoning the Community for Counsel."

27 Not only are the members to listen to the abbot or prioress, but these monastic leaders are also to listen to the members. All are responsible for the community. Monasteries today use consent by ballot of the whole monastery in making important decisions.

28 Benedict is most likely referring to the newer members of the community.

29 Benedict asks for humility, that is, the understanding that my idea may be good but it is not the only idea. Benedict cautions against presumption, a term he uses often in the Rule in connection with going against the prioress or abbot.

30 Throughout the Rule Benedict carefully explains how the prioress and abbot are to conduct themselves as leaders.

~ I like Benedict's reminder to listen to the new kid on the block. When I worked at AT&T years ago, a bright, creative woman came to our work group. Peggy's ideas were met with closed ears and grumbling: "What does she know? She just got here." Benedict puts the words of a new person into a spiritual realm—what he or she says could be at the direction of the Holy Spirit. Benedict is showing that these words often come through the most unlikely speaker, reminding us to be open in our own listening.

As often as anything important is to be done in the monastery, the prioress or abbot shall call the whole community together and explain what the business is; and after hearing the advice of the members, let the prioress or abbot ponder it and follow what they judge the wiser course.[27] The reason why we have said all should be called for counsel is that the Spirit often reveals what is better to the younger.[28] The community members, for their part, are to express their opinions with all humility, and not presume to defend their own views obstinately.[29] The decision is rather the prioress' or the abbot's to make, so that when the abbot or prioress of the community has determined what is more prudent, all must obey. Nevertheless, just as it is proper for disciples to obey their teacher, so it is becoming for the teacher to settle everything with foresight and fairness.[30]

CHAPTER 3. SUMMONING THE COMMUNITY FOR COUNSEL, 1–6

31 Benedictine monk and scholar Terrence Kardong points out that by using the word "all" Benedict expands these instructions for members taken from the Rule of the Master to also include the abbot and prioress. The power and authority of the abbot and prioress is then balanced by their own adherence to the Rule (Kardong).

32 A goal of monastic life is to replace personal will with God's will as it is expressed through the abbot or prioress and through the Rule itself.

33 Presumption is linked to defiance of the superior. "Discipline of the rule" occurs frequently throughout the Rule, leading us to think that Benedict has a fixed system of punishment for various offenses. While he provides specifics in some cases, such as grumbling, I believe that he left the specifics of discipline to the wisdom and compassion of the prioress or abbot. The Latin word *disciplina* can also mean "learning," which to me is the real purpose of Benedict's discipline—to encourage a positive change in actions.

≈ We have a hard time not following the desire of our heart. "Isn't the desire of my heart God's will for me?" we might ask. Benedict knows that this desire can be self-centered and not in the best interests of the community. The Rule becomes the check against this. Benedict also frees the monastic so that he or she can focus all energies on actually *seeking* God, clearing away decisions you and I encounter on a daily basis: Should I do *A* or should I do *B*? Instead the stance becomes that of listening: What does the Rule call me to do? What does the community ask of me? What does the prioress ask me to do? Obedience actually brings freedom.

34 We will discover other places in the Rule where Benedict reminds the prioress and abbot that they will need to give an accounting of their decisions and actions to God. Yet judgment need not be feared, Benedict assures, for God is just.

≈ When we are with another person—a son or daughter, a co-worker, a spouse, a partner, or even a friend—do we ever consider that we might need to give an accounting to God of how we acted and what we said? How would it make a difference if we thought this were true?

Accordingly in every instance, all are to follow the teaching of the rule, and no one shall rashly deviate from it.[31] In the monastery, monastics are not to follow their own heart's desire,[32] nor shall they presume to contend with the prioress or abbot defiantly, or outside the monastery. Should any presume to do so, let them be subjected to the discipline of the rule.[33]

CHAPTER 3. SUMMONING THE COMMUNITY FOR COUNSEL, 7–10

Moreover, the prioress or abbot must themselves reverence God and keep the rule in everything they do; they can be sure beyond any doubt that they will have to give an account of all their judgments to God, the most just of judges.[34]

CHAPTER 3. SUMMONING THE COMMUNITY FOR COUNSEL, 11

35 Benedict does not want members of his community to suffer, so when the monastic finds a task is too difficult, dialogue with the superior is possible. The member approaches the prioress or abbot with consideration and respect, without emotional overtones or a prideful manner. Because of obedience, there is no outright refusal.

36 In recognition of the voice of Christ in the abbot or prioress, the monastic will do the task if that is the decision of the superior, and will turn to God for help.

37 There is a much different flavor in chapter 68 of the Rule than in chapter 5, where Benedict asks for prompt and unquestioning obedience. Chapter 68 shows Benedict's consideration and understanding of people—some things may be beyond a person's capabilities. Indirectly it also seems to say that perhaps on occasion the superior may be inaccurate in his or her assessment of what a brother or sister can do. Many scholars feel that this chapter was added later in Benedict's life when he was influenced by Augustine. Perhaps Benedict learned that dialogue can make for a more harmonious community.

Chapter 68 reminds us to always approach people with respect and consideration. There are times when we may need to bide our time until the other person can give us their full attention. Finally, others may have a better understanding of what we can do and challenge us to grow as we do what at first seems impossible.

Monastics may be assigned a burdensome task or something
they cannot do. If so, they should, with complete
gentleness and obedience, accept the order given them.
Should they see, however, that the weight of the burden
is altogether too much for their strength, then they should
choose the appropriate moment and explain patiently to
the prioress or abbot the reasons why they cannot perform
the task. This they ought to do without pride, obstinacy or
refusal.[35] If after the explanation the abbot or prioress is still
determined to hold to their original order, then the junior
must recognize that this is best. Trusting in God's help, she
or he must in love obey.[36]

CHAPTER 68.[37] ASSIGNMENT OF IMPOSSIBLE TASKS, 1–5

The Vow of *Conversatio,* Conversion of Life

38 The third Benedictine vow is *conversatio,* which also appears as *conversatio morum.* Both are difficult to translate into English and have resulted in extensive scholarly pondering and debate. The term *conversatio,* meaning "way of life," is often used in Christian literature to translate the Greek *askēsis,* the ancient root of our word "ascetic." Benedict uses *conversatio* for "the monastic life" (Fry). We can also think of it as "the Christian life." When lived faithfully and fervently, both the monastic life and the Christian life will bring growth and transformation. While the whole Rule points to conversion of life, Benedict does not make frequent references to the vow.

39 Benedict states that *conversatio*—translated here in Prologue 49 as "this way of life"—is a progression that includes both faithfulness (stability) and following God's instructions and teachings (obedience). The goal is sharing in the eternal presence. Benedict sees monastic life as a progression toward purity of heart, virtue, and salvation.

⟳ Reflecting on my own life, I can relate to the way one monk described the monastic life: "We fall down, and we get up again. We fall down, and we get up again." Monastic life and the Christian life progress toward greater and greater likeness of Christ.

40 Benedict links the adjective "holy" to the monastic way of life.

41 Deans take care of small groups of monastics.

42 At the beginning of chapter 73, the last chapter in the Rule, Benedict once again connects virtue and *conversatio,* the monastic life.

But as we progress in this way of life[38] and in faith, we shall run on the path of God's commandments, our hearts overflowing with the inexpressible delight of love.[39]

PROLOGUE 49

If the community is rather large, some chosen for their good repute and holy life[40] should be made deans.[41]

CHAPTER 21. DEANS OF THE MONASTERY, 1

The reason we have written this rule is that, by observing it in monasteries, we can show that we have some degree of virtue and the beginnings of monastic life.[42]

CHAPTER 73. THIS RULE ONLY A BEGINNING OF PERFECTION, 1

Embracing the Vows

43 We see all three vows in action in chapter 58, where Benedict explains the process for receiving new members. Benedict needs to know if those desiring entrance are on a quest for shelter, food, and safety or on a quest for God.

44 Benedict wants to test the sincerity of potential members as well as give them a taste for things to come—a life that requires patience and steadfastness, stability and obedience. We may find this length of time unreasonable but Benedict was actually moderate. Fifth-century abbot John Cassian notes that it took ten days at the door of an Egyptian monastery before gaining entry. Prospective members endured insults and injuries while they followed the instruction to embrace the knees of all the brothers passing by (Cassian). The repetitions of "if" in chapter 58 show us how much emphasis Benedict places on the actions and decisions of the newcomer.

45 For the first time in monasticism, the term "novice" is used to indicate a prospective member. Benedict is also the first monastic legislator to arrange for special novitiate quarters, where newcomers would live for a year. American monasteries no longer segregate the novices to any great extent (Kardong) and certainly do not keep the women and men knocking on the door for five days. One knock will do.

Do not grant newcomers to the monastic life an easy entry, but, as the apostle says, "Test the spirits to see if they are from God" (1 John 4:1).[43] Therefore, if someone comes and keeps knocking at the door, and if at the end of four or five days has shown patience in bearing harsh treatment and difficulty of entry, and has persisted in the request, then that one should be allowed to enter and stay in the guest quarters for a few days.[44] After that, the person should live in the novitiate, where the novices study, eat and sleep.[45]

CHAPTER 58. THE PROCEDURE FOR RECEIVING MEMBERS, 1–5

46 For Benedict, a "senior" is not an elderly person but whoever came to the monastery before another. If you arrived today and I arrive next week, you would be senior to me. That a senior with gifts for spiritual guidance looks after all novices reveals the very personal way Benedict helps newcomers in their quest for God.

47 Once again Benedict wants to make sure that the novice is sincere and eager for monastic life. Two critical pieces of monastic life are mentioned—obedience and the Divine Office.

48 Life in the monastery is not easy. Everyone needs to be on the same page, as we would express it today. Benedict wants to make sure novices are intent on doing all that is necessary to become solid members of the community. A big part of this is giving up one's self-direction. Novices turn their lives over to the prioress or abbot, the Rule, and the other members. The goal is to conform to God's will as expressed through the community. That people join a monastic community does not make them immediately able to let go of ego and pride or make it easy to do what is asked of them. That is hard, difficult, and lifelong work.

49 Stability is required from day one. The Rule will be read several times so that novices clearly understand the norms of the community that they must follow in obedience. In these three verses alone, "if" is repeated four times. Until they are received as members, novices are free to leave *if* they choose to do so.

50 Benedict's novitiate lasts about a year. Today it is most often a number of years with preliminary vows being taken before the final vow, as described here by Benedict. In these verses Benedict addresses both obedience and stability.

51 Here the novice promises to live the Benedictine vows of stability, fidelity to monastic life (*conversatio*, or conversion of life), and obedience. The promise is written in a document that the novice signs and lays on the altar. The novice prays for God's help and then asks for prayers from each member of the community.

A senior chosen for skill in winning souls should be appointed to look after the newcomer with careful attention.[46] The concern must be whether the novice truly seeks God and shows eagerness for the Opus Dei, for obedience and for trials.[47] The novices should be clearly told all the hardships and difficulties that will lead to God.[48]

CHAPTER 58. THE PROCEDURE FOR RECEIVING MEMBERS, 6–8

If they promise perseverance in stability, then after two months have elapsed let this rule be read straight through to them, and let them be told: "This is the law under which you are choosing to serve. If you can keep it, come in. If not, feel free to leave." If they still stand firm, they are to be taken back to the novitiate, and again thoroughly tested in all patience.[49]

If after due reflection they promise to observe everything and to obey every command given them, let them then be received into the community. But they must be well aware that, as the law of the rule establishes, from this day they are no longer free to leave the monastery.[50]

When they are to be received, they come before the whole community in the oratory and promise stability, fidelity to the monastic life, and obedience.[51]

If they have any possessions, they should either give them to the poor beforehand or make a formal donation of them to the monastery, without keeping back a single thing for themselves, well aware that from that day they will not

(continued on page 91)

|52| The monastics free themselves of possessions and are clothed in what belongs to the monastery.

|53| Another "God forbid," showing Benedict's utter horror at turning back on one's vows and soul.

|≈| When new people come to our faith communities, we may not be clear on the expectations or requirements. Even if we have these, we may fear that if these are shared, people will vanish. We tend to approach entrance into our communities as a matter of public relations—we make ourselves inviting to others. Benedict offers another way: provide guidance, educate, encourage, and then ask for a commitment. When we welcome people into our faith communities we can take these steps but know that the real choice each person makes is to choose God.

|54| Benedict never underestimates the challenge of monastic life and gives allowances for difficulty in making a final decision.

|55| Many scholars think that this was the concluding verse of an earlier version of the Rule (Kardong). But no matter, Benedict wants the Rule to always be foremost in the minds of his monastics. Today, portions of the Rule are read each day in the monastery following a prescribed pattern created by the Order of St. Benedict. Books and online resources can help us keep the Rule foremost in our own minds as well. For example, Joan Chittister's *The Rule of St. Benedict: A Spirituality for the 21st Century* offers both the Rule text and her insightful reflections for each day's reading.

|≈| A word as the chapter draws to a close. All of us are seekers of fulfillment, meaning, love, and God. Women and men in religious life can be models for us through their faithfulness and obedience to their uniquely lived Christian life, guided by the Rule that shows them the path to God.

have even their own body at their disposal.[52] The clothing taken from them is to be put away and kept safely in the wardrobe, so that, should they ever agree to the devil's suggestion and leave the monastery—which God forbid— they can be stripped of the clothing of the monastery before they are cast out.[53]

CHAPTER 58. THE PROCEDURE FOR RECEIVING MEMBERS, 9–11, 14–15, 17, 24–25, 27–28

If any community members, following their own evil ways, leave the monastery but then wish to return, they must first promise to make full amends for leaving. Let them be received back, but as a test of humility they should be given the last place. If they leave again, or even a third time, they should be readmitted under the same conditions. After this, however, they must understand that they will be denied all prospect of return.[54]

CHAPTER 29. READMISSION OF MEMBERS WHO LEAVE THE MONASTERY, 1–3

We wish this rule to be read often in the community, so that none of the members can offer the excuse of ignorance.[55]

CHAPTER 66. THE PORTER OF THE MONASTERY, 8

Community Organization and Norms

1 Rank by time of entry organizes the community and helps members know their place in relation to others. A member is both a senior to some and a junior to others. This minimizes reasons for discord or confusion and maximizes opportunities for respectful interactions. Although Benedict was not the first to structure his community in this way—Pachomius also used this structure—his plan was truly revolutionary for the time. Society was stratified socially and economically, but none of this counted when a person entered Benedict's community. A noble who entered in the afternoon would be junior to a poor man who entered that morning. A facet of Benedictine humility is the recognition that one person is not better than anyone else. For the noble, being junior to a poor person was an opportunity to practice humility for all are equal in Christ (Galatians 3:28).

2 Benedict thinks highly of virtue and goodness of life. He considers them criteria for leadership as well as for changing rank.

3 Benedict shows concern about altering the rank of members. Changes in community rank have the potential to cause discord. He is also vigilant about the misuse of authority by the superior—changes could be based on favoritism or spite. And so to encourage fairness and integrity, Benedict cautions the prioress and abbot to always remember that they are ultimately responsible to God for whatever they do. This caution appears frequently in the Rule.

4 Whether Benedict ever mentions the Eucharistic Mass is open to scholarly dispute. Some scholars feel that Communion was taken daily with a full Mass on Sundays (Kardong). The emphasis in the Rule is on the Divine Office.

4 □ Cultivating Love

Benedictine Relationships and Community

The Rule of Benedict is a manual for creating caring and respectful relationships and community. We are all a part of many different communities—family, friendships, church community, workplace, volunteer organizations, and so forth. For me, Benedict's ideas ring true for all. In this chapter we will see how Benedict structures community and addresses interactions between community members. As you read, think about what Benedict recommends that would be helpful and life-giving in your own relationships and communities.

Monastics keep their rank in the monastery according to the date of their entry,[1] the virtue of their lives,[2] and the decision of the prioress or abbot. The prioress or abbot is not to disturb the flock entrusted to them nor make any unjust arrangements, as though they had the power to do whatever they wished. They must constantly reflect that they will have to give God an account of all their decisions and actions.[3] Therefore, when the members come for the kiss of peace and for Communion,[4] when they lead psalms or stand in choir, they do so in the order already existing among them or decided by the abbot or prioress. Absolutely nowhere shall age automatically determine rank. Remember that Samuel and Daniel were still boys

(continued on page 95)

5 Benedict supports his statement regarding age with scripture.

〜 Most monastic communities today do not follow the hierarchy described here or stress seniority (Kardong).

6 What a beautiful verse. Respect and love bind members together.

7 Addressing one another as Benedict suggests binds the community together in a familial closeness and honors tenure. Benedict asks for respect for elders in the community and a deeper respect for the abbot or prioress, who represents Christ in the monastery.

8 Again, a caution to the abbot or prioress.

〜 Today we are casual with names, calling most people by their first names regardless of age, with the exceptions of perhaps doctors, clergy, professors, and high-ranking public officials. I wonder what it would be like to follow Benedict's plan for addressing others, for example, in my church community. This would probably be a welcome relief for people who have trouble remembering names but it does not seem to be Benedict's motivation. However we address others, love and respect can form the attitude of the heart.

9 Another way that members show respect is supported by a quote from Romans that appears again in chapter 72 of the Rule. Scholars are not sure whether rank in the monastery or chronological age is referred to here.

〜 I recall the first time that anyone got up and offered me a seat in the subway. While the offer was kind, thoughtful, and touchingly respectful, I knew I was no longer in my prime!

when they judged their elders (1 Sam. 3; Dan. 13:44–62).[5] Therefore, apart from those mentioned above whom the abbot or prioress have for some overriding consideration promoted, or for a specific reason demoted, all the rest should keep to the order of their entry. For example, someone who came to the monastery at the second hour of the day must recognize that they are junior to someone who came at the first hour, regardless of age or distinction.

CHAPTER 63. COMMUNITY RANK, 1–8

The younger monastics, then, must respect their elders, and the elders must love their juniors.[6] When they address one another, no one should be allowed to do so simply by name: rather, the elders call the younger "sister" or "brother" and the younger members call their elders "nonna" or "nonnus," which is translated as "venerable one." But the abbot and prioress, because we believe that they hold the place of Christ, are to be called "abbot" or "prioress" not for any claim of their own, but out of honor and love for Christ.[7] They for their part must reflect on this and in their behavior show themselves worthy of such honor.[8]

CHAPTER 63. COMMUNITY RANK, 10–14

When older members come by, the younger ones rise and offer them a seat, and do not presume to sit down unless the older bids them. In this way, they do what the words of scripture say: "They should each try to be the first to show respect for the other" (Rom. 12:10).[9]

CHAPTER 63. COMMUNITY RANK, 16–17

10 In addition to asking for love and respect among members, Benedict also addresses situations that could result in a fractious community. Here he states that *every* precaution must be taken and that "in no way whatsoever" should defense of another be done. As chapter 69 was added to the Rule later, perhaps he encountered this situation with its unpleasant consequences. Again, to presume means that the monastic has taken on unauthorized authority.

~ Blood ties can be strong but so can friendship. Defense can result in cliques that divide the community as members take sides. "There are few social problems more dangerous than this in a cenobitic community" (Kardong). Or in any community, I will add. While it is important to speak up on another's behalf concerning an injustice, we need to be discerning in both word and action.

11 Another caution against unauthorized actions.

12 Benedict uses scripture to illustrate and reinforce this manner of discipline. His hope is to deter monastics from harmful behavior that will endanger their souls.

13 Benedict draws from the wisdom of scripture in an appeal for reasonable actions toward others.

~ While physical punishment is not condoned in our culture, we have ways of punishing others beyond our authority to do so. We use the subtler forms—unkind words, silence, disapproving looks, and even verbal berating. When tempted toward these actions, let's instead practice patience, understanding, forgiveness, and reconciliation.

Every precaution must be taken that one member does not presume in any circumstance to defend another in the monastery or to be their champion, even if they are related by the closest ties of blood. In no way whatsoever shall monastics presume to do this, because it can be a most serious source and occasion of contention.[10] Anyone who breaks this rule is to be sharply restrained.

CHAPTER 69. THE PRESUMPTION OF DEFENDING ANOTHER IN THE MONASTERY, 1–4

In the monastery every occasion for presumption is to be avoided, and so we decree that no one has the authority to excommunicate or strike any member of the community unless given this power by the prioress or abbot.[11] "Those who sin should be reprimanded in the presence of all, that the rest may fear" (1 Tim. 5:20).[12]

If any member, without the command of the abbot or prioress, assumes any power over those older or, even in regard to the young, flares up and treats them unreasonably, let that one be subjected to the discipline of the rule. After all, it is written: "Never do to another what you do not want done to yourself" (Tobit 4:16).[13]

CHAPTER 70. THE PRESUMPTION OF STRIKING ANOTHER MONASTIC AT WILL, 1–3, 6–7

14 With the stipulation of "far away," perhaps monks from neighboring monasteries were not as welcome. Benedictine monk and scholar Timothy Fry explains that there is ample evidence in early monastic literature that male monastics visited other communities to learn more about the spiritual life (Fry). Abbots also traveled to conferences. Women made up a considerable portion of religious travelers during late antiquity (fourth through ninth centuries) (Dietz). While residing both inside and outside monastic communities, women traveled to visit holy sites, sought out holy women and men, and visited or established monasteries (Dietz). Marthana, a leader of a fourth-century monastic community in Syria at the eastern end of the Mediterranean Sea, may have seen travel and meeting holy people as part of her monastic vocation (Dietz). Benedict's sister, Scholastica, a nun, visited her brother yearly.

15 While providing generous hospitality, Benedict also sets boundaries to preserve a calm environment.

16 Benedict believes that God's hand is in all of life and so advises the abbot or prioress to be open to suggestions made in humility and love by visitors. An abbot or prioress today may ask a visiting monastic for observations (Kardong).

~ In my visits to monasteries I meet monastics from other communities and often from overseas. Monastic women and men are travelers and often write about their experiences. For a wonderful account of monastic travel, see Albert Holtz, *Pilgrim Road: A Benedictine Journey Through Lent,* rev. ed. (New York: Morehouse Publishing, 2015).

~ Making suggestions can be especially tempting in family situations. But Benedict says, "In a flood of words you will not avoid sin" (Proverbs 10:19 and RB 6.4). I will add to this, "you will not avoid alienating your family."

Visiting monastics from far away will perhaps present themselves and wish to stay as guests in the monastery.[14] Provided that they are content with the life as they find it, and do not make excessive demands that upset the monastery, but are simply content with what they find, they should be received for as long a time as they wish.[15] They may, indeed with all humility and love, make some reasonable criticisms or observations, which the prioress or abbot should prudently consider; it is possible that God guided them to the monastery for this very purpose.[16]

CHAPTER 61. THE RECEPTION OF VISITING MONASTICS, 1–4

17 Character counts. Benedict knows that an individual can influence a community in both positive and negative ways. He is protective of his community. Benedict's beautiful statement of unity reflects an important attitude of his monastic community toward members of other communities. As mentioned in the Prologue, Benedictines today reach out through interfaith dialogue.

〰 In Benedict's day the abbot or prioress had the authority to ask a troublesome monastic to leave and the person, while probably not pleased, would comply. Monastic communities today also encounter monastic and non-monastic visitors who may be excessively demanding or have psychological problems. One sister shared that "monastic communities will put up with a lot today," but it is not uncommon to ask persons who are excessively demanding to leave. A book of services is available to help individuals find housing or needed assistance; they are not just told to leave. Monastics planning to visit another monastery, even for a short stay, might be asked to send a letter from their superior attesting to their character.

At work, in church or other groups, or when volunteering we can find ourselves with a person whom we view as troublesome. Helpful instructions in the Rule can guide us in a challenging situation, like putting the love of Christ first (RB 4.21) and bearing with the greatest patience the weakness of others (RB 72.5). We also might consider the monastic practice of seeking self-knowledge to learn why we are bothered.

18 Discipline in private or before the whole community is used to maintain cohesiveness, respect, and order in the community as well as to protect the soul of the monastic. A common disciplinary measure is excommunication—exclusion from leading a psalm or response, or from community prayers, meals, or working with others.

19 Unless the task is otherwise delegated, discipline is the responsibility of the abbot or prioress. Discipline varies according to the individual and is done with moderation. The goal of discipline is to bring the person back into full communion with the group. It is done in a spirit of love, to help them grow in obedience and humility.

But if during their stay they have been found excessive in their demands or full of faults, they should certainly not be admitted as a member of the community. Instead, they should be politely told to depart, lest their ways contaminate others.

If, however, they have shown that they are not the kind of persons who deserve to be dismissed, let them, on their request, be received as a member of the community. They should even be urged to stay, so that others may learn from their example, because wherever we may be, we are in the service of the same God.[17]

CHAPTER 61. THE RECEPTION OF VISITING MONASTICS, 6–7, 8–10

There ought to be due proportion between the seriousness of a fault and the measure of excommunication or discipline.[18] The prioress or abbot determines the gravity of faults.[19]

CHAPTER 24. DEGREES OF EXCOMMUNICATION, 1–2

20 To make satisfaction—to make amends—a member is to acknowledge fault and carry out imposed penalties. Making satisfaction repairs damage done by an inappropriate action toward an individual or the whole community. The concern is with both exterior actions and interior attitudes such as pride or anger that brought about the action. Through satisfaction the monastic's relationship is restored with others as well as with God (Fry). Making amends concerns repentance, reconciliation, and forgiveness.

21 Such exclusion from important community activities would undoubtedly be difficult for members who have pledged their lives to the community.

〰 I heard a monk once say that Benedict's instructions for discipline offer us nothing today whether we live inside or outside a monastery. While it is true that the Rule contains outmoded practices such as excommunication, the underlying goal is still valid—to help the monastic amend actions for the better and to preserve harmony in the community. While the chapters on discipline have been called the penal code, they are more accurately named "the healing code" (Böckmann), reflecting the true intent of Benedict's discipline.

Today the abbess or abbot provides help for monastics who are angry or acting out of resistance to monastic life. Psychological counseling, conversation within the community, and speaking with a mature member who has struggled with the challenges of monastic life are ways that a member is offered healing and an opportunity to begin again.

Benedict's practice of discipline is both firm and compassionate, characteristics that we can model whenever we need to discipline others. As leaders, supervisors, or parents, we can, like Benedict, have the goals of restoring an individual to community and helping them to take another step forward in personal growth.

22 Notice how Benedict uses Jesus's image of physician as a model for the abbot or prioress to heal a struggling member. Benedict asks for the greatest possible love and attention in order to save the member's soul.

23 The Latin *senpectae* is found nowhere else in Christian literature and scholars debate its meaning. Some suggest that it means a mustard paste (Fry), which gives a beautiful image of the *senpectae*'s function in healing a monastic sister or brother. Made from mustard seed and water, warmed mustard plaster is spread between two dressings or towels and placed on the body, such as the chest, where it draws out the infection. Benedict explains the personal qualities and actions of these monastic healers who seek to draw out the infection within the wavering sister or brother. Wisdom, experience in the monastic life, and love guide the *senpectae* as they urge the monastic to be restored to right relationship with God and community.

The role of *senpectae* continues in today's monasteries. The door is not shut on a hurting or self-alienating member. A superior today would not hesitate to send a member for psychological help or even to one of the places specifically set up for monastics who have addictions. The abbot or prioress would also speak with the member privately. If another monastic has a good relationship with the struggling member, he or she may be asked to step in as *senpectae*. Many of us outside the monastery have been helped by *senpectae*. Spiritual directors, life coaches, and trusted friends have guided us toward a change of heart and healing.

24 Prayer is important and discipline is done for the good of the individual as well as for the community.

25 The monastic leader is to act quickly and thoughtfully to bring back a straying member. As the vicar of Christ in the monastery, the abbot or prioress is to follow the example of Christ the Shepherd and have love at the root of all actions.

26 Benedict modifies scripture here in a way that shows his love for the straying sheep—adding "mercifully"—and his deep love for Christ—adding "sacred" to "shoulders."

The abbot and prioress must exercise the utmost care and concern for the wayward because "it is not the healthy who need a physician, but the sick" (Matt. 9:12).[22] Therefore they ought to use every skill of a wise physician and send in *senpectae*, that is, mature and wise members who, under the cloak of secrecy, may support the wavering sister or brother, urge them to be humble as a way of making satisfaction, and "console them lest they be overwhelmed by excessive sorrow" (2 Cor. 2:7).[23] Rather, as the apostle also says: "Let love be reaffirmed" (2 Cor. 2:8), and let all pray for the one who is excommunicated.[24]

It is the responsibility of the abbot or prioress to have great concern and to act with all speed, discernment and diligence in order not to lose any of the sheep entrusted to them. They should realize that they have undertaken care of the sick, not tyranny over the healthy. Let them also fear the threat of the prophet in which God says: "What you saw to be fat you claimed for yourselves, and what was weak you cast aside" (Ezek. 34:3–4). They are to imitate the loving example of Christ, the Good Shepherd, who left the ninety-nine sheep in the mountains and went in search of the one sheep that had strayed.[25] So great was Christ's compassion for its weakness that "he mercifully placed it on his sacred shoulders"[26] and so carried it back to the flock (Luke 15:5).

CHAPTER 27. THE CONCERN OF THE ABBOT AND PRIORESS
FOR THE EXCOMMUNICATED, 1–4, 5–9

‿ Benedictines use a compassionate approach to discipline that stresses transformation and reconciliation. They do not focus on blame but on restoration. Approaching discipline with this Benedictine mind-set can help us discern life-giving ways to help a wavering sister or brother, a beloved child of God, be restored to the fold.

27 Prayer will draw the community together and encourage the monastic being disciplined to make amends and change in the future.

28 Benedict is not concerned with discipline for the sake of penalizing someone who does not follow the "common rule of the monastery" (RB 7.55). Benedict's aim is for the individual to recognize a fault or inappropriate action or word, to feel sorrow for his or her action, to accept the discipline, and, most importantly, to amend actions in the future. An important part of the discipline is to initiate the desire for healing by acknowledging one's error before the community and asking for forgiveness. Sin erodes our relationship with God and others. Satisfaction is to make these relationships right again.

‿ Ever get sent to bed without dinner? I did—once. This exclusion gave me a concrete picture of my need to do better in thought and action and an opportunity to begin again. See "Opening Our Eyes to the Light from God," Prologue 35–38 and the unnumbered note "Although not in the Rule ..." Although we are not required to prostrate ourselves at the feet of spouses, partners, children, friends, and supervisors, the idea of clearing the air is excellent. I do not recall any air-clearing after my event of excommunication from the table. Perhaps a quick read of the Rule then would have given me the idea to make satisfaction. ("Gee, I'm sorry, Mom and Dad.") I continue to make mistakes at home—an unkind remark, an inappropriate action (shutting doors too firmly on occasion), not listening. Under Benedict's plan I would spend lots of time on the floor! But I am blessed with an understanding and good-humored spouse and have learned the value of making satisfaction.

Those excommunicated for serious faults from the oratory and from the table are to prostrate themselves in silence at the oratory entrance at the end of the celebration of the Opus Dei. They should lie face down at the feet of all as they leave the oratory, and let them do this until the prioress or abbot judges they have made satisfaction. Next, at the bidding of the prioress or abbot, they are to prostrate themselves at the feet of the prioress or abbot, then at the feet of all that they may pray for them.[27] Only then, if the prioress or abbot orders, should they be admitted to the choir in the rank the prioress or abbot assigns. Even so, they should not presume to lead a psalm or a reading or anything else in the oratory without further instructions from the prioress or abbot. In addition, at all the hours, as the Opus Dei is being completed, they must prostrate themselves in the place they occupy. They will continue this form of satisfaction until the prioress or abbot again bids them cease.

Those excommunicated for less serious faults from the table only are to make satisfaction in the oratory for as long as the prioress or abbot orders. They do so until they give them blessing and say: "Enough."[28]

CHAPTER 44. SATISFACTION BY THE EXCOMMUNICATED, 1–8, 9–10

~ Perhaps Benedict knew that a fault or accident not declared might be a burden on the heart that becomes a distraction. Honesty is needed in community and admitting mistakes or errors is a part of this honesty.

29 In contrast to making public satisfaction, Benedict is sensitive to the need for privacy concerning personal matters. Psychological causes for actions need not be shared with everyone. Declaring these to the abbot, prioress, or spiritual elder is enough. Wise guides can shepherd the individual toward healing. Notice that the abbot or prioress seeks the assistance of others.

~ To confess a mistake or error and talk about it with a trusted person are two actions that have brought me peace of heart and growth in maturity. Admitting a mistaken word or inappropriate action, uncomfortable as it can be, strengthens my relationships. Sharing actions and thoughts with David, my life coach, continues to help me discover and heal old wounds.

If monastics commit a fault while at any work—while
working in the kitchen, in the storeroom, in serving, in the
bakery, in the garden, in any craft or anywhere else—either
by breaking or losing something or failing in any other
way in any other place, they must at once come before the
prioress or abbot and community and of their own accord
admit their fault and make satisfaction. If it is made known
through another, they are to be subjected to a more severe
correction.

When the cause of the sin lies hidden in the conscience,
the monastic is to reveal it only to the prioress or abbot or
to one of the spiritual elders, who know how to heal their
own wounds as well as those of others, without exposing
them and making them public.[29]

CHAPTER 46. FAULTS COMMITTED IN OTHER MATTERS, 1–4, 5–6

30 If the monastic does not reform ("God forbid!" Benedict exclaims over such a dreaded condition in RB 28.2), the prioress or abbot is to act as a wise physician, taking the steps Benedict describes in verses 3–8. With the good of the whole community in mind, the monastic who refuses to amend is asked to leave.

⟩ Although we may disagree with some actions, Benedict's discipline reminds us that a goal of discipline is to reunite a healed individual with the community and to trust God to help in this process.

31 Compare what Benedict says in the verses from chapter 30 with those from chapter 70 on page 113. The latter verses added to the Rule later show a moderation in severity of treatment.

After applying compresses, the ointment of encouragement, the medicine of divine scripture, and finally the cauterizing iron of excommunication and strokes of the rod, if they then perceive that their earnest efforts are unavailing, let them apply an even better remedy: they and all the members should pray for them so that God, who can do all things, may bring about the health of the sick one. Yet if even this procedure does not heal them, then finally, the prioress or abbot must use the knife and amputate. For the apostle says: "Banish the evil one from your midst" (1 Cor. 5:13); and again, "If the unbeliever departs, let that one depart" (1 Cor. 7:15), "lest one diseased sheep infect the whole flock."[30]

CHAPTER 28. THOSE WHO REFUSE TO AMEND AFTER FREQUENT REPROOFS, 3–8

Every age and level of understanding should receive appropriate treatment. Therefore, as often as the young, or those who cannot understand the seriousness of the penalty of excommunication, are guilty of misdeeds, they should be subjected to severe fasts or checked with sharp strokes so that they may be healed.[31]

CHAPTER 30. THE MANNER OF REPROVING THE YOUNG, 1–3

In the oratory and at table, the young are kept in rank and under discipline. Outside or anywhere else, they should be supervised and controlled until they are old enough to be responsible.

CHAPTER 63. COMMUNITY RANK, 18–19

〜 I like Benedict's use of age-appropriate discipline. Physical punishment does not sit well with me but this kind of discipline was used in Benedict's time. He must have felt that such measures were necessary until the child was old enough to understand and feel remorse for faults and misdeeds. His motivation in all his disciplinary measures was the ultimate saving of the individual's soul.

Cultivating Respect and Love

32 Modeling the important themes in the Rule of mutual respect and love, Benedict gives ample opportunity to reach the oratory in time. See also "Turning to God," RB 13.2 and note 3.

〜 I like the way Benedict offers consideration for others by saying the psalm slowly. I think we could all look for ways to cut people some slack and give them some compassionate help along the way.

33 Being late has consequences, not because the instructions in the Rule for promptness were not followed but because worship, the community, and God were not respected. Therefore, Benedict is firm here, encouraging members to change their behavior. This practice of standing in last place has been dropped in most monasteries today.

〜 Have you ever been at a meeting and had to wait for someone? What if this person was habitually late? Being late impacts the cohesiveness and harmony of a group and may reveal a person's lack of real commitment to the group. A number of years ago, a supervisor told me that if I start to be late to our meetings, it is a sign that I really do not want to be there. Perhaps Benedict knew this, too. Benedict addresses disrespectful behavior directly. Are we firm enough today when encountering disrespectful behavior? Perhaps calling such actions to a person's attention in a spirit of love and reconciliation is in order.

34 Idle talk instead of listening to the Word of God in the oratory gives an opening for the evil one to distract people from God with meaningless conversation. Benedict has the soul of the member in his heart and encourages the monastic to attend the Divine Office.

The young up to the age of fifteen should, however, be carefully controlled and supervised by everyone, provided that this too is done with moderation and common sense.

CHAPTER 70. THE PRESUMPTION OF STRIKING ANOTHER
MONASTIC AT WILL, 4–5

If at Vigils monastics come after the Doxology of Psalm 95, which we wish, therefore, to be said quite deliberately and slowly,[32] they are not to stand in their regular place in choir. They must take the last place of all, or one set apart by the prioress or abbot for such offenders, that they may be seen by them and by all, until they do penance by public satisfaction at the end of the Opus Dei. We have decided, therefore, that they ought to stand either in the last place or apart from the others so that the attention they attract will shame them into amending.[33] Should they remain outside the oratory, there may be those who would return to bed and sleep, or, worse yet, settle down outside and engage in idle talk, thereby "giving occasion to the evil one" (Eph. 4:27; 1 Tim. 5:14). They should come inside so that they will not lose everything and may amend in the future.[34]

CHAPTER 43. TARDINESS AT THE OPUS DEI OR AT TABLE, 4–9

35 Tardiness at meals has serious consequences. Without everyone there the prayer before the meal cannot be said. The same exclusion from the common table applies if someone leaves before the closing prayer after the meal. Benedict adds another unpleasant consequence for tardiness or skipping out early—no wine! I wonder if that helped encourage punctuality.

Eating together binds a community—sharing a meal is a sacred event. To be late is to disavow the community and its sacred time. The community meal is a "primary symbol of the very life and unity of the group [cenobitic life]; when it is disrupted by inconsiderate or chaotic behavior, there is a threat to the common good that cannot be ignored or condoned" (Kardong). Most monastic communities today continue prayer together before and after meals.

A meal where all family members are present is rare today. What are the consequences of families not sitting down together to share a meal? With smartphones and tablets, so many families sit together but really are not present to one another; they choose to be absorbed in their technology rather than talking with each other. Benedict reminds us of the importance of simply sharing a meal together. The impacts go far beyond the actual meal into the health, cohesiveness, and mutual love within whatever the community might be.

But, if monastics do not come to table before the verse so that all may say the verse and pray and sit down at table together, and if this failure happens through their own negligence or fault, they should be reproved up to the second time. If they still do not amend, let them not be permitted to share the common table, but take their meals alone, separated from the company of all. Their portion of wine should be taken away until there is satisfaction and amendment. Anyone not present for the verse said after meals is to be treated in the same manner.[35]

CHAPTER 43. TARDINESS AT THE OPUS DEI OR AT TABLE, 13–17

36 Monastic writers before Benedict caution against eating in between meals. Meals are to be taken in community, not as sole individuals whenever the whim strikes. A reminder that the word "presume" implies that the nibbler has gone against the authority of the prioress or abbot.

37 I have puzzled over this verse, wondering why amends were required just for refusing something from the superior. Perhaps it is this: since the prioress or abbot is a representative of Christ in the community, then refusing something from this person is refusing something from Christ. One writer spoke of the refusal as "the failure to respond to the grace of the moment" (Kardong).

〰 I love to nibble and fail miserably at verse 18. Moreover, offer me a cookie—I will never refuse.

〰 One way that monastics show respect for one another and cultivate love is by maintaining silence as directed in the Rule. We looked at selections about silence in the Rule in chapter 2. For the Rule text and annotations about silence, please see "Turning to God," RB 42.1, 8–9 and notes 56 and 57; RB 52.1–5 and notes 58–59; and also RB 48.5 and note 61.

No one is to presume to eat or drink before or after the time appointed.[36] Moreover, if anyone is offered something by the prioress or abbot and refuses it, then, if the monastic later wants what was refused or anything else, that one should receive nothing at all until appropriate amends have been made.[37]

CHAPTER 43. TARDINESS AT THE OPUS DEI OR AT TABLE, 18–19

38 The Rule of the Master views the sick suspiciously as perhaps not *really* being sick but wanting a break from the routine. In contrast, Benedict elevates care of the sick to first place because serving the sick is actually serving Christ. He states the need for care three times in this chapter and the admonition against neglect twice. More than serving the sick, which is important, care is an expression of love.

39 Benedict presents care of the sick as a spiritual practice, as he does with so many other tasks. Those who tend the sick are serving the Lord and will gain a greater reward in their salvation. The sick can experience spiritual growth as they accept their weakness and trust God for their care and healing. Mutual love and respect bond caregiver and care receiver together and both are responsible to keep the other from sadness or anger.

40 Because of the spiritual importance of serving the sick, the abbot or prioress is to be not simply careful but "*extremely* careful" to ensure proper attention. "The warm and intense Christian care for the sick" prescribed in the Rule "caused the Benedictine monasteries to become centers of sick-care and medicinal progress in the following centuries" (Lentini).

41 Noted Benedictine monk and scholar Adalbert de Vogüé calls chapter 36 "one of the best-written in the Rule. It is as practical as it is spiritual, a chapter such as one finds in no other Rule" (de Vogüé).

〰 Caregiving is difficult and exhausting. Being sick is relentless, discouraging, and even frightening. As life presents both roles to us, remembering the spiritual aspects as Benedict describes can lighten our burden and give us hope.

Care of the sick must rank above and before all else so that they may truly be served as Christ who said: "I was sick and you visited me" (Matt. 25:36), and, "What you did for one of these least of my people you did for me" (Matt. 25:40).[38]

Let the sick on their part bear in mind that they are served out of honor for God, and let them not by their excessive demands distress anyone who serves them. Still, the sick must be patiently borne with, because serving them leads to a greater reward.[39] Consequently, the prioress or abbot should be extremely careful that they suffer no neglect.[40]

CHAPTER 36.[41] THE SICK, 1–3, 4–6

42 The prior (male monastery) or subprioress (female monastery) is second-in-command to the abbot or prioress.

43 The Rule's chapter 5 focuses on obedience to the prioress or abbot. Here in chapter 71, written later in his life, Benedict expands that obedience to all members of the community. Obedience is the spiritual discipline of listening and responding. Obedience is a blessing because it draws members closer to God and salvation; it is also a gift given to one another. Notice that the way the obedience is to be carried out is important enough to be mentioned by Benedict—"all love and concern."

~ Imagine a family, workplace, community, or church where everyone practices mutual obedience, listening to the needs of others and responding in love. A number of years ago I was in a synchronized swim group where the women did just that but none of us knew about the Rule, including me. In this challenging sport, each member supported the other, listened carefully as new routines were taught, and, for the more experienced swimmers, patiently taught skills to the newer members. We truly cared about one another. This group has become my model "Benedictine" community.

Obedience is a blessing to be shown by all, not only to the prioress and abbot but also to one another, since we know that it is by this way of obedience that we go to God. Therefore, although orders of the prioress and abbot or of the subprioress or prior[42] appointed by them take precedence, and no unofficial order may supersede them, in every other instance younger members should obey their elders with all love and concern.[43] Anyone found objecting to this should be reproved.

CHAPTER 71. MUTUAL OBEDIENCE, 1–5

44 Once again, Benedict takes steps to preserve peace and harmony in the community. The importance of making satisfaction is under-scored by the stiff punishment. Stubbornly refusing to make amends is a serious matter for it indicates lack of obedience to the Rule and to the demands of the community (Kardong). It takes courage to go to another person seeking to make amends but this action can keep negative feelings from escalating.

〰 While I can see the importance of taking steps to preserve open and honest relationships, being expelled from the monastery (RB 71.9) seems extreme. It also seems not to track with a more compassionate Benedict revealed elsewhere in the Rule. Even so, these verses give us a way to preserve love in relationships. When I think that I have done something to disturb my husband or feel he may be upset with me (or I with him), I will initiate a discussion. I have done this with others as well, a direct result of remembering Benedict's instructions in this chap-ter. The discussion and, if needed, my apology, calms our emotions before unaddressed anger and resentment build an impenetrable wall.

〰 Listen up! In chapter 72 Benedict offers a model of who we can be at home or in any community or relationship. In his usual fashion, Benedict gives solid, scripture-based actions to promote harmony and encourage love.

45 Of Greek derivation and used frequently in the New Testament in either a positive or negative sense, "zeal" in classical times could mean "jealousy," "rivalry," "passion," "ambition," and "fervor" (Fry). It is a word full of drive and energy.

46 Good zeal impacts the community in positive ways, but it is first and foremost, for Benedict, a spiritual discipline that has eternal consequences.

If a member is reproved in any way by the abbot or prioress or by one of the elders, even for some very small matter, or gets the impression that one of the elders is angry or disturbed with them, however slightly, that member must, then and there without delay, fall down on the ground at the other's feet to make satisfaction, and lie there until the disturbance is calmed by a blessing. Anyone who refuses to do this should be subjected to corporal punishment or, if stubborn, should be expelled from the monastery.[44]

CHAPTER 71. MUTUAL OBEDIENCE, 6–9

Just as there is a wicked zeal[45] of bitterness which separates from God and leads to hell, so there is a good zeal[46] which separates from evil and leads to God and everlasting life.

CHAPTER 72. THE GOOD ZEAL OF MONASTICS, 1–2

47 Good zeal is fostered by not just any love but by "fervent" love, also translated as "warmest" love. Remember that this kind of love is not necessarily a fuzzy feeling but one that seeks the best for another.

48 In verse 4 Benedict begins his list of what good zeal looks like in action, turning to the apostle Paul for a key ingredient. I have included several alternate words in the Rule text in brackets. Using an image from games and races, members are to compete with one another in trying to be the first to show respect. What if we try this in our relationships? I believe it would be transformative.

People usually think that life in a monastery is all prayers and peace. But Benedictine Terrence Kardong shares this reality: "Cenobitic life is precisely a lifetime exercise in patience" (Kardong). Let's add to that family life or any relationship where we are in close and continual contact with others. I try hard to remember this verse when I am growing impatient with others. Our Lord had plenty of patience. I ask him to help me nurture mine.

49 An alternate translation: "No one should pursue what he judges advantageous to himself, but rather what benefits others" (Kardong). The spiritual life in the monastery is not about focusing all the attention on the self. "The willingness and desire to do whatever is useful for the community is perhaps the most valuable trait in a cenobitic monk. It is the practical face of love in a community that calls itself the body of Christ." For the most part, "spiritual progress comes about indirectly through going out to the other in love" (Kardong).

50 Chapter 72 presents mutual love as the deepest meaning of the cenobitic life. "The monastic enterprise without love is a cold charade" (Kardong).

≈ Not only do verses 3–7 show us the way to good relationships and community but they also show us a path to a peace-filled heart. Our natural inclination and self-will may incline us to do the opposite of what Benedict is saying; for example, to become frustrated and angry over the weaknesses of others. From my own experience, this is a

(continued on page 126)

This, then, is the good zeal which members must foster with fervent love:[47] "They should each try to be the first to show respect to the other" (Rom. 12:10), supporting [bearing] with the greatest [utmost, inexhaustible] patience one another's weaknesses of body or behavior, and earnestly competing in obedience to one another.[48] No monastics are to pursue what they judge better for themselves, but instead, what they judge better for someone else.[49]

CHAPTER 72.[50] THE GOOD ZEAL OF MONASTICS, 3–7

closed-hearted, tight-fisted, self-centered focus that is far from a heart of peace. The next time we get impatient with someone, let's promise to put these verses into action.

〰️ In the final verses of chapter 72, Benedict zeros in on where his monastics are to show love.

51 "Let them prefer nothing whatever to Christ" is a direct quote from the influential early Christian writer Cyprian (d. 258 CE), who added, "for he has preferred nothing to us" (Kardong).

52 Eternal life is the goal of monastic life and with good zeal in their hearts shown in actions, the monastics will be guided there by Christ.

〰️ For me, the entire Rule is summed up in chapter 72, verse 11: "Let them prefer nothing whatever to Christ." To prefer Christ means that what we say and what we do are guided by our preference for him. With minor exceptions of outmoded practices, all that Benedict suggests in the Rule are ways we can live preferring nothing to Christ. What might each of us do in this moment to act from our preference for Christ? Perhaps a prayer of gratitude is a way to begin.

Among themselves they show the pure love of sisters and brothers; to God, reverent love; to their prioress or abbot, unfeigned and humble love. Let them prefer nothing whatever to Christ,[51] and may Christ bring us all together to everlasting life.[52]

CHAPTER 72. THE GOOD ZEAL OF MONASTICS, 8–11

1 These tools and indeed the entire Rule are all about love: love of God, love of neighbor, and love of self. And so it is not surprising that Benedict begins the list of tools with the Great Commandment found in the three synoptic Gospels.

2 The Bible is the primary resource for the tools found in the Rule of the Master, whether quoted exactly by Benedict or drawn from and paraphrased. Benedict retained this emphasis on Holy Scripture.

5 □ Living with Integrity and Virtue

The Tools for Good Works

Basing the Rule's chapter 4, "The Tools for Good Works," on the Rule of the Master, Benedict offers seventy-four "tools of the spiritual craft" (RB 4.75) to help monastics acquire virtue. These tools foster harmony in relationships, integrity in personal life, health in physical life, and intentionality in the search for God. Lists of tools such as Benedict's were common in the early Church and used by monastic writers to show that they wished to bind the monastic movement to the Church (Kardong).

Our eyes can glaze over when faced with such a long list of suggested actions. Cistercian monk Michael Casey states a truth: "Overwhelmed, most of us are inclined to set our minds on cruise control and simply glide through the list without paying too much attention to its details" (Casey). Why not instead opt for a listening heart (Prologue 1)? I think you will discover these tools can help you live a compassionate and meaningful life.

First of all, "love God with your whole heart, your whole soul and all your strength, and love your neighbor as yourself"[1] (Matt. 22:37–39; Mark 12:30–31; Luke 10:27).[2]

CHAPTER 4. THE TOOLS FOR GOOD WORKS, 1–2

3 Benedict includes five of the Ten Commandments that are most applicable to members of a monastic community.

4 Benedict changes "father and mother" to include everyone in the monastic community.

5 This version of the Golden Rule is used elsewhere in the Rule (RB 61.14; RB 70.7).

∼ Denying oneself and curbing bodily cravings through discipline are ways that monastics turn from self to God and God's will.

6 Benedict chooses scripture carefully. In the section of 1 Corinthians from which these words are drawn, Paul is talking about the self-control and discipline needed for running a race to win. Monastics are running a race to win eternal life. See "Opening Our Eyes to the Light from God," Prologue 13, 22, 44, and 49, and notes 13, 23, 35, and 40.

7 Fasting is an important spiritual discipline. A goal for monastics is to do all things with love, not just because the Rule requires a certain action. We can assume that this applies to all the tools that Benedict gives us in this chapter.

∼ The four tools found in verses 10–13 present a huge challenge. We are inclined to want things a certain way, one that is comfortable for us. Fasting for me is infrequent (Benedict would ask me to amend this). When I do fast, however, it makes me more reliant on God because my body and brain slow down. I experience in a tiny and temporary way the tragic gnawing hunger that so many in our world encounter every day of their lives. Fasting increases my compassion for people who do not have sufficient food or water for themselves or for their families and encourages my ongoing support of organizations that seek to alleviate hunger.

Then the following: "You are not to kill, not to commit adultery; you are not to steal nor to covet" (Rom. 13:9); "you are not to bear false witness" (Matt. 19:18; Mark 10:19; Luke 18:20).[3] "You must honor everyone"[4] (1 Peter 2:17), and "never do to another what you do not want done to yourself" (Tobit 4:16; Matt. 7:12; Luke 6:31).[5]

CHAPTER 4. THE TOOLS FOR GOOD WORKS, 3–9

"Renounce yourself in order to follow Christ" (Matt. 16:24; Luke 9:23); "discipline your body"[6] (1 Cor. 9:27); do not pamper yourself, but love fasting.[7]

CHAPTER 4. THE TOOLS FOR GOOD WORKS, 10–13

8 Benedict weaves familiar biblical imperatives with other acts of compassion. He asks monastics to model Jesus by helping others, continuing a tradition that began in early monasticism. In the belief that their gifts were a spiritual sacrifice to Christ, ancient monasteries would offer "an immense quantity of provisions and food" to those in need (Cassian).

9 The Rule is centered in Christ and shows how to follow Christ in daily life. These two verses express this central principle. The love of Christ can be looked at in two ways: first, a Christlike love for others guiding our actions, thoughts, and words; and second, our own love of Christ being more important than anything else.

Verses 20–21 are among my favorites in the Rule because they give clarity to what it means to follow Christ—to love through Christ and from Christ. When I am able to remember these words in the heat of the moment, they help me turn toward Christ and away from the emotion that is pulling me from living by Benedict's tools.

You must relieve the lot of the poor, "clothe the naked, visit the sick" (Matt. 25:36), and bury the dead. Go to help the troubled and console the sorrowing.[8]

CHAPTER 4. THE TOOLS FOR GOOD WORKS, 14–19

Your way of acting should be different from the world's way; the love of Christ must come before all else.[9]

CHAPTER 4. THE TOOLS FOR GOOD WORKS, 20–21

~ In verses 22–28 Benedict shows us how to put the love of Christ first. These seven tools support harmony in relationships and peace in the community, both of which Benedict cares about a great deal. They are ways to be transparent to others; to be honest, truthful, and loving. Here we find echoes of Jesus's Sermon on the Mount (Matthew chapters 5–7).

10 Benedict is not saying not to be angry but rather to not let anger drive our actions. I like this translation, too: "Do not act under the impulse of anger" (Kardong).

11 Benedict cautions against unexpressed anger that can grow into a deep-seated resentment.

12 A tool for honesty that begins in the heart, the source of love. Benedict reinforces the need for truth from the heart in verse 28. See note 14 below.

13 A hollow greeting of peace is an empty greeting, lacking sincerity and care. I think Benedict would tolerate a bland greeting better than one with fake sincerity. Members of a community must trust one another and that includes trusting that the person before you is acting as he or she feels or thinks rather than putting up a smoke screen of propriety.

14 While echoing Jesus's instructions to not take an oath (Matthew 5:34–37), Benedict reminds monastics that in a community of mutual openness, strong statements are not required and that communication has a direct route from the heart to the mouth, and then to the ear of the other person (Casey). Benedict encourages his community to allow for differences of opinion and gently held views. "Opinionated bombast is not unknown in monasteries, but it rarely serves a useful purpose" (Casey).

You are not to act in anger[10] or nurse a grudge.[11] Rid
your heart of all deceit.[12] Never give a hollow greeting of
peace[13] or turn away when someone needs your love. Bind
yourself to no oath lest it prove false, but speak the truth
with heart and tongue.[14]

CHAPTER 4. THE TOOLS FOR GOOD WORKS, 22–28

～ Being truthful, transparent, and gentle in speech are not readily found in our world. Benedict values these characteristics because they are trust builders, especially when they are offered with the guidance of love. No one has to figure out a person's *real* opinion or hidden agenda. I had a parishioner who followed Benedict's directions here. While I did not always like what I heard, I always knew where I stood. I felt relaxed and free in her presence.

～ Benedict gives tools to use when in conflict or struggling with others. The tools found in verses 29–33 put into action the monastic directive found in the Prologue: "Let peace be your quest and aim" (Prologue 17).

15 While not quoting scripture directly, Benedict's instruction to bless instead of curse clearly expresses New Testament teaching on reconciliation. Verse 33 is from the Beatitudes: "Blessed are those who are persecuted for righteousness' sake, for theirs is the kingdom of heaven" (Matthew 5:10).

～ I invite you to reread RB 4.20–33. Which practices would bring peace to your relationships and heart?

"Do not repay one bad turn with another" (1 Thess. 5:15;
1 Peter 3:9). Do not injure anyone, but bear injuries
patiently. "Love your enemies" (Matt. 5:44; Luke 6:27). If
people curse you, do not curse them back but bless them
instead.[15] "Endure persecution for the sake of justice"
(Matt. 5:10).

CHAPTER 4. THE TOOLS FOR GOOD WORKS, 29–33

16 Of the eight troublesome thoughts, pride is the most difficult to crush. See "Turning to God," note 47 for a list of these thoughts. Monastics can become prideful over their spiritual achievements.

17 These three verses address excess, not an occasional overeating or oversleeping. Monastics of Benedict's day believed that an excess of wine and food could bring on lustful thoughts. A focus on wine, food, sleep, or lolling about could also become substitutes for a focus on God. Benedict asks his monastics to take care of their bodies as well as their souls, and to practice moderation in eating and sleeping.

18 In a number of places Benedict cautions against the fine art of grumbling. He does not call it that but we can, through practice, raise our discontented murmuring to that level. "There are few things Benedict likes less than grumbling" (Kardong). Grumbling about people or situations to ourselves or to others is detrimental to relationships and community. Speaking ill of others is not living with the love of Christ first (RB 4.21). For additional admonitions against grumbling, see "Seeking God," RB 5.14–19 and notes 24–26.

〰 Verses 34–40 remind me that some things that I think are great may be damaging to body and mind when done in excess. And some things, like grumbling, need not be done at all.

19 Benedict places these reassuring words almost at the physical center of chapter 4, "The Tools for Good Works." He reminds us that we do not have to do all this alone. God is with us and will help us.

〰 Ahhh. I put my trust in what Benedict says here and repeat it like a mantra—as did the monastics of old—as a way to stay on course and not be derailed by the evil one. What a wonderful reminder to trust God. Just saying this verse brings me peace of heart.

"You must not be proud,[16] nor be given to wine" (Titus 1:7;
1 Tim. 3:3). Refrain from too much eating or sleeping, and
"from laziness" (Rom. 12:11).[17] Do not grumble or speak ill
of others.[18]

CHAPTER 4. THE TOOLS FOR GOOD WORKS, 34–40

Place your hope in God alone.[19]

CHAPTER 4. THE TOOLS FOR GOOD WORKS, 41

20 Once again Benedict distances himself from the Pelagians, who believed that human beings were capable of choosing good and evil without God's help. Instead, Benedict follows Augustine's belief and that of the Church that humanity needs the intervention of God's grace. We are to take responsibility for the wrongs done and not succumb to the temptation of blaming someone else for that which we have created on our own.

21 Benedict wants his community to remember that each person will be accountable to God for the way he or she lived. As we have seen, he is also very clear that the goal is everlasting life and that the Rule, the abbot or prioress, and the community all facilitate this goal. Benedict wants his community to yearn for everlasting life with a totality of being—body, mind, and spirit. Such yearning motivates monastics to use the seventy-four tools of the spiritual craft as means to this end.

Because the desire for God will only be satisfied in eternity, monastic life turns each member's gaze from the present toward that final goal. "Everything that happens in this present life, including our occasional foretasting of the reality that awaits us, is meant to keep us walking along the road that leads to eternal life. This means keeping alive our faith, our hope, and our ardent desire" (Casey).

There is a beautiful window in my church that depicts the Annunciation, when the angel Gabriel comes to Mary and announces that she will bear the Son of God and name him Jesus (Luke 1:26–38). Her image, kneeling as she reads scripture, arms crossed on her chest in an attitude of humility, has become a visual picture of my own desire for God.

If you notice something good in yourself, give credit
to God, not to yourself, but be certain that the evil you
commit is always your own and yours to acknowledge.[20]

CHAPTER 4. THE TOOLS FOR GOOD WORKS, 42–43

Live in fear of the day of judgment and have a great horror
of hell. Yearn for everlasting life with holy desire.[21]

CHAPTER 4. THE TOOLS FOR GOOD WORKS, 44–46

22 Benedict includes this tool to help his community realize that time is limited; they must be energetic to amend faults. Also, remembering death can help us to live, now.

23 Our first reaction here may be negative. Is God a critical judge just waiting for a mistake, like a critical parent or an unreasonable supervisor? This is not Benedict's intention. While he wants personal vigilance, knowing that God's gaze is upon us can also give us hope. We are not alone. See RB 4.41 and note 19 above.

24 Benedict asks for self-awareness to be able to immediately notice wrongful thoughts. It takes practice. See "Opening Our Eyes to the Light from God," note 28. To further help let go of wrongful thoughts, monastics share them with wise spiritual guides. This is one of the many places in the Rule that reveal Benedict to be an excellent sixth-century psychologist.

~ Awareness, awareness, awareness. Most people do not realize how much this has been stressed in monastic life since the time of the Desert Fathers and Mothers. Awareness is a spiritual practice that I work at to increase my self-knowledge. In contemporary terms, I grow more aware of my hot buttons so that they do not drive the bus (that is, control my actions). I try to recognize them right when they appear. I then tell them to get out of the driver's seat and I banish them to the back of the bus, where they can stew over their loss of power.

Day by day remind yourself that you are going to die.[22]
Hour by hour keep careful watch over all you do, aware
that God's gaze is upon you, wherever you may be.[23] As
soon as wrongful thoughts come into your heart, dash them
against Christ and disclose them to your spiritual guide.[24]

CHAPTER 4. THE TOOLS FOR GOOD WORKS, 47–50

25 Benedict now presents cautions for speech that stress both honesty and seriousness in the monastic pursuit.

26 Benedict asks for generosity in conversation with others. "When we fall in love with the sound of our own voice and are amazed at the wisdom that flows from our mouths, we so fill the available space around us that others are pushed to the margins. As a result, they are forced to become passive listeners to our not-so-thrilling monologues" (Casey).

27 "Do not engage in empty babbling or joking" (Kardong) describes exactly what Benedict wants his community to avoid—meaningless and shallow talk, guffawing and harmful speech. These actions distract speaker and listener from the path toward God and disrupt the environment of the monastery.

28 Notice that Benedict does not say, "do not laugh." He is cautioning against excessive and loud laughter that we know can become a constant disruption. Saying or doing things just to get a laugh is also drawing attention to oneself and is to be avoided by monastics.

～ Benedict includes prayer in the tools for good works. We looked at these verses in chapter 2 of this book. See "Turning to God," RB 4.55–58 and notes 33 and 34.

29 To allow God's will to replace personal will requires turning from the limited voice of the self to God.

30 Another "God forbid!" The horror for Benedict is an abbot or prioress who does not practice what he or she preaches. Benedict quotes Jesus to reinforce the need for obedience.

31 This is Benedict's only mention of "chastity." Chastity is a work of grace that takes a long time to acquire. It relies on acquiring other virtues such as patience and restraint of anger. The early Christian theologian John Cassian writes at length about this quality. He describes a sexual restraint that makes chastity possible. Chastity will bring tranquility to the soul when sexual temptations are silenced (Casey).

Guard your lips from harmful or deceptive speech.[25] Prefer moderation in speech[26] and speak no foolish chatter,[27] nothing just to provoke laughter; do not love immoderate or boisterous laughter.[28]

CHAPTER 4. THE TOOLS FOR GOOD WORKS, 51–54

"Do not gratify the promptings of the flesh" (Gal. 5:16); hate the urgings of self-will.[29] Obey the orders of the prioress and abbot unreservedly, even if their own conduct—which God forbid—be at odds with what they say. Remember the teachings of the Holy One: "Do what they say, not what they do" (Matt. 23:3).[30]

CHAPTER 4. THE TOOLS FOR GOOD WORKS, 59–61

Do not aspire to be called holy before you really are, but first be holy that you may more truly be called so. Live by God's commandments every day; treasure chastity.[31]

CHAPTER 4. THE TOOLS FOR GOOD WORKS, 62–64

32   Benedict offers tools that support peace in community and relationships by turning from attitudes and actions that are confrontational. While quarreling would have happened in the monastery as in any community or family, Benedict cautions against enjoying it, which could make it habitual.

33   Another meaning of *fugere* is "to run away from" or "to flee." Benedict often uses such action-packed words to encourage swift action.

34   Direction for both juniors (RB 4.70) and seniors (RB 4.71). When Benedict uses the word "young" (*iuniores*) he generally means those who are junior in the community regardless of age.

〰️ We can read verses 65–73 and think, "Right. I'll follow all that." But the truth is, unless we are self-aware, we can slip easily into the negative behaviors Benedict lists and resist doing the positive ones. To me, verse 73 is a great illustration of RB 4.21: "The love of Christ must come before all else."

35   The list of tools to practice is long and each tool requires intention and practice. Benedict reminds monastics and us that God will give the grace to work toward fulfilling all the tools for good works and will be forgiving when the mark is missed.

36   Benedict reinforces that the tools are not just to be read but also to be used unceasingly in daily life. Benedict uses the image of a worker receiving wages—a heavenly reward—for a job well done. We encountered this image of the worker in the Prologue. See "Opening Our Eyes to the Light from God," Prologue 14.

〰️ We might not think that all the Tools for Good Works are spiritual practices because we might not consider that actions like eating, quarreling, or laughing have spiritual consequences. Benedict asks us to expand our thinking and realize that *everything* we do positively or negatively impacts our relationship with God and others. This is why these tools are spiritual craft and not just a list of commendable actions.

Harbor neither hatred nor jealousy of anyone, and do nothing out of envy. Do not love quarreling;[32] shun[33] arrogance. Respect the elders and love the young.[34] Pray for your enemies out of love for Christ. If you have a dispute with someone, make peace with that person before the sun goes down.

CHAPTER 4. THE TOOLS FOR GOOD WORKS, 65–73

And finally, never lose hope in God's mercy.[35]

CHAPTER 4. THE TOOLS FOR GOOD WORKS, 74

These, then, are the tools of the spiritual craft. When we have used them without ceasing day and night and have returned them on the day of judgment our wages will be the reward God has promised:[36] "What the eye has not seen nor the ear heard, God has prepared for those who love God" (1 Cor. 2:9).

CHAPTER 4. THE TOOLS FOR GOOD WORKS, 75–77

37 Perseverance is needed to use these seventy-four tools day after day. Knowing the challenge for the monastic and the Christian, Benedict ends his chapter with a call for an unceasing commitment to place and people. It is in community, with these tools at hand to "guard the heart and open the soul to the Holy" (Chittister), that we will become people whose hearts overflow with the "inexpressible delight of love" (Prologue 49).

Restraint of Speech

38 In chapter 6 of the Rule Benedict expands upon the need for moderation in speech (RB 4.52–53). Why restrain speech? Restraining speech has biblical roots, as Benedict illustrates in these verses.

39 The junior needs to be silent to listen and learn from the elders. The vow of obedience asks the monastic to listen to the superior and other members of the community as well as to avoid saying hurtful words or fueling one's pride. Restraining speech helps monastics curb grumbling. Benedict is not saying to avoid speech altogether but that restraint shows respect for others.

40 Benedict reminds members to honor the superior because he or she represents Christ in the monastery.

Wow! For those of us who love to talk this is a) tough to read, b) tougher to understand, and c) perhaps impossible to do. We all want to share our good words, right? Yet sometimes we are so eager to jump in with our two cents' worth that we totally miss what the other person is saying. Benedict offers an anti-competition stance in conversation: we need not talk all the time.

While the phrase "silence is golden" would have appealed to Benedict, monasteries today do not hold to such strictness regarding speech. Women and men in monastic community strive to respect and listen to one another, the message of this chapter we can take to heart. Let's practice non-speaking more often. By restraining our words we will be free to share the love of Christ before all else (RB 4.21).

The workshop where we are to toil faithfully at all these tasks is the enclosure of the monastery and stability in the community.[37]

Chapter 4. The Tools for Good Works, 78

Let us follow the prophet's counsel: "I said, I have resolved to keep watch over my ways that I may never sin with my tongue. I was silent and was humbled, and I refrained even from good words" (Ps. 39:2–3). Here the prophet indicates that there are times when good words are to be left unsaid out of esteem for silence. For all the more reason, then, should evil speech be curbed so that punishment for sin may be avoided. Indeed, so important is silence that permission to speak should seldom be granted even to mature disciples, no matter how good or holy or constructive their talk, because it is written: "In a flood of words you will not avoid sin" (Prov. 10:19); and elsewhere, "The tongue holds the key to life and death" (Prov. 18:21).[38] Speaking and teaching are the teacher's task; the disciple is to be silent and listen.[39]

Therefore, any requests to an abbot or prioress should be made with all humility and respectful submission.[40]

Chapter 6. Restraint of Speech, 1–6, 7

41 Monastics are to have high standards when it comes to speaking. "Vulgarity" is based on the Latin word *scurra*, which means "a rough fellow who loitered about the streets telling tasteless jokes" (Kardong). A great picture of what Benedict does not want.

42 The talk described here is inappropriate for the person on the journey to God; it is a distraction. "The mouth is like the door of an inner cloister. St. Benedict wants the door closed to certain kinds of speech" (Fry). Here is a translation that emphasizes Benedict's concern: "As for crude jokes and idle talk aimed at arousing laughter, we put an absolute clamp on them in all places. We do not permit the disciple to so much as open his mouth for such talk" (Kardong).

∾ While we understand the benefits of laughter today, tasteless jokes are still not appropriate.

We absolutely condemn in all places any vulgarity[41] and gossip and talk leading to laughter, and we do not permit a disciple to engage in words of that kind.[42]

CHAPTER 6. RESTRAINT OF SPEECH, 8

6 □ Choosing Truth

Humility in the Rule

In the fourth century, hermit John of Lycoplis said, "And so, my children, first of all let us discipline ourselves to attain humility, since this is the essential foundation of all virtues" (Russell). In the twenty-first century, Benedictine sister Joan Chittister wrote, "The Rule of Benedict spends only three paragraphs on obedience—thought by many moderns to be the arch-virtue of the spiritual life. But Benedict has nineteen paragraphs on humility. No doubt about it: he was trying to get our attention" (Chittister).

Will Benedict get our attention?

Humility is not a sought-after personal quality and is generally mis-understood. We often think humility means humiliation and weakness. But Jesus called himself humble in heart and promised rest for those car-rying heavy burdens (Matthew 11:28–20). The heavy burden we carry is ourselves—our drive to get what we want, our belief that we are always right, our self-focus. Humility—its root meaning "earth"—grounds us in the truth of who we are. It helps us accept ourselves and others and allow life to unfold around us without the struggle to continually change things. Humility enables us to bend to God's way instead of being entrenched in our own way. We become better able to see God's direction for us through scripture and other resources, the circumstances of our life, and the guidance of others (obedience).

In chapter 7 of the Rule Benedict describes the process of achieving humility as climbing a ladder with twelve steps. Each rung of the ladder represents an aspect of humility. I will provide an alternate wording from the tenth anniversary revised edition of my book *St. Benedict's Toolbox: The Nuts and Bolts of Everyday Benedictine Living* to clarify each step.

1 Benedict uses scripture to describe what humility looks like in action. Self-exaltation is pride, the opposite of humility. We think we are better than others, and our ideas are better than others. On the other hand, "humility joins us with the rest of the human race" (Casey); we live truthfully with a realistic view of ourselves and others.

2 From the Latin verb meaning "to shout" or "to yell," showing the urgent need to heed scripture and pursue humility.

3 We can instead have our eyes on self-promotion or look for ways to let others see our "greatness."

4 Benedict connects humility with the goal of eternal life. He calls for a humble heart that God will raise to heaven. Jacob's dream in Genesis 28:12 was a favorite image of early monastic writers such as Basil (Kardong).

5 Step 1: "To accept that God is present in my life and to live from that awareness" (Tomaine).

Steps on the ladder are not to be considered a strict sequential progression. However, the first step, the constant recollection of the presence of God, is the foundation on which all the other steps rest.

Sisters and Brothers, divine Scripture[1] calls[2] to us saying:
"Whoever exalts themselves shall be humbled, and whoever
humbles themselves shall be exalted" (Luke 14:11; 18:14).
In saying this, therefore, it shows us that every exaltation
is a kind of pride, which the prophet indicates has been
shunned, saying: "O God, my heart is not exalted; my eyes
are not lifted up and I have not walked in the ways of the
great nor gone after marvels beyond me" (Ps. 13:1).[3]

CHAPTER 7. HUMILITY, 1–3

Accordingly, if we want to reach the highest summit of
humility, if we desire to attain speedily that exaltation in
heaven to which we climb by the humility of this present
life, then by our ascending actions we must set up that
ladder on which Jacob in a dream saw "angels descending
and ascending" (Gen. 28:12). Without doubt, this descent and
ascent can signify only that we descend by exaltation and
ascend by humility. Now the ladder erected is our life
on earth, and if we humble our hearts God will raise it to
heaven. We may call our body and soul the sides of this
ladder, into which our divine vocation has fitted the various
steps of humility and discipline as we ascend.[4]

CHAPTER 7. HUMILITY, 5–9

The first step of humility, then, is that we keep "the
reverence of God always before our eyes" (Ps. 36:2) and
never forget it.[5]

CHAPTER 7. HUMILITY, 10

6　For discussions of hell and judgment, see "Opening Our Eyes to the Light from God," Prologue 5–7 and note 10, and Prologue 42–44 and the unnumbered note "I understand eternal life …"

7　Lists of sins attached to human beings' physical aspects were common in the writing of the theologians in the early Church.

8　Key ideas and themes in the Rule appear in verses 11–13: reverencing God; the goal of eternal life; obedience; mindfulness of one's thoughts, actions, and will; and the ever-present gaze of God of which one Benedictine quipped, "There is no vacation from God" (Kardong).

〰️　Humility confronts us in our weakness and reminds us that "we need to do battle if we are to remain upright…. Christian life is a struggle" (Casey). Constant self-awareness is a line of defense against the wiles of the devil. Accepting God's presence in our lives, which is the first step of humility, helps us draw on God's presence for guidance.

〰️　In verses 14–30, not included here, Benedict again stresses that God sees all and that we must be "vigilant every hour" (RB 7.29) in order to avoid sin. God also searches the heart and mind (RB 7.14). A final caution is that sometimes what people think is right plunges them "into the depths of hell" (Proverbs 16:25 in RB 7.21).

We must constantly remember everything God has
commanded, keeping in mind that all who despise God will
burn in hell for their sins, and all who reverence God have
everlasting life awaiting them.[6] While we guard ourselves at
every moment from sins and vices of thought or tongue, of
hand or foot, of self-will or bodily desire,[7] let us recall that
we are always seen by God in the heavens, that our actions
everywhere are in God's sight and are reported by angels at
every hour.[8]

CHAPTER 7. HUMILITY, 11–13

9 Step 2: "To make doing God's will my prime directive" (Tomaine).
Basil wrote that those who set out to do God's will must ultimately turn from their own will (Kardong). Monastics turn to God's will through the practice of obedience. Again Benedict points to following Christ's actions.

~ Things are becoming a bit more challenging here. I like doing what I want to do and can get confused as to what God's will *really* is for each moment of my life. If you feel that way too, we can take a clue or two from Benedictine obedience. Our first step is to "cherish Christ above all" (RB 5.2). Our second step is to be responsive, caring, and patient with the people God places in our life, as the brother or sister is to the prioress or abbot and to other community members (RB 5.7–9 and RB 72.6). The apostle Paul provides a final step that I have found meaningful:

> Rejoice always, pray without ceasing, give thanks in all circumstances; for this is the will of God in Christ Jesus for you. Do not quench the Spirit. (1 Thessalonians 5:16–18)

Amen!

10 Step 3: "To recognize that I cannot always be in control, and to listen and respond to those who are—to be obedient" (Tomaine).
Love of God and the imitation of Jesus are the motivations for obedience to one's superiors.

~ Most of us like to be in control. Yet there are times when we need to step back and be guided by others or the circumstances of our lives. While we may not have an abbot or prioress, we have people to whom we are responsible—spouses, partners, supervisors, friends, children. We can listen and respond to their needs out of the love of God and in imitation of Jesus.

The second step of humility is that we love not our own
will nor take pleasure in the satisfaction of our desires;
rather we shall imitate by our actions that saying of
Christ's: "I have come not to do my own will, but the will of
the One who sent me" (John 6:38).[9]

CHAPTER 7. HUMILITY, 31–32

The third step of humility is that we submit to the prioress
or abbot in all obedience for the love of God, imitating
Jesus Christ of whom the apostle says: "Christ became
obedient even to death" (Phil. 2:8).[10]

CHAPTER 7. HUMILITY, 34

11　Step 4: "To be patient and steadfast when our obedience places us in a difficult or unfair situation" (Tomaine).

What monastics may feel are injustices may be personal feelings of being wronged that can spring from the desire to control people or situations. Dealing with situations that seem unfair are opportunities for growth in the monastic life (conversion of life).

12　The Latin word Benedict uses here is *patientiam*, meaning "patience." Patience is an important aspect of humility in community and relationships. Trust in God is what makes patience possible. Benedict asks for patience in other areas of the Rule: bearing injuries (RB 4.30), caring for the sick (RB 36.5), speaking with the superior (RB 68.2), supporting one another's weakness of body or behavior (RB 72.5), sharing the sufferings of Christ (Prologue 50), and seeking entrance to the community (RB 58.11). The monastic accepts suffering as an opportunity to practice humility. I like that Benedict brings in the heart, the place where our own suffering can be healed by God's love.

〰️　While we may recognize the importance of doing God's will and taking direction from another, this step can really challenge us. "We are to endure even an unjust situation?" we ask. Well, yes and no. We tend to evaluate everything in terms of its benefit to us. What we think is difficult or unjust may be an opportunity to practice patience and set our self-will aside. Clearly if a situation is dangerous or demeaning, a change needs to happen. But often what we struggle against is something that does not line up with what we want.

The fourth step of humility is that in this obedience under difficult, unfavorable, or even unjust conditions,[11] our hearts quietly[12] embrace suffering and endure it without weakening or seeking escape. For scripture has it: "Anyone who perseveres to the end will be saved" (Matt. 10:22), and again, "Be brave of heart and rely on God" (Ps. 27:14). They are so confident in their expectation of reward from God that they continue joyfully and say, "But in all this we overcome because of Christ who so greatly loved us" (Rom. 8:37).

CHAPTER 7. HUMILITY, 35–37, 39

13 Step 5: "To practice self-disclosure with someone I trust" (Tomaine).
Sharing thoughts with a superior, elder, or spiritual guide is a long-standing practice in monasticism. The routine of monastic life, regular and perhaps relentless in its sameness, creates an environment where "hidden aspects of the personality become manifest" (Casey). By sharing thoughts, monastics have a better understanding of themselves, which is a goal that supports personal and spiritual growth. Benedict reminds his community of the need for prayer and reliance on God's faithfulness.

～ Having had counselors to help me get through some tough times—supervisors during my years of parish work and now a life coach—it is easy for me to accept this step of humility. But I often find it challenging to share personal thoughts and struggles. Yet when I share, the door of my heart opens to greater self-knowledge and the healing wisdom of others. When I accept that I am not perfect, I stand firmly on this step of humility.

14 Step 6: "To be willing to do the most menial tasks and be at peace with them" (Tomaine).
Imagine a sixth-century noble entering the monastery who is asked to wash the floor, a task that, outside the monastery, would be performed by a servant or a slave. Benedict instructs monastics to let go of that part of themselves that thinks they are too important to do such a task. Instead, accept the reality of life as it comes. *This* is humility.

15 Wow! Benedict sounds demeaning here. Who wants a menial task? Who considers themselves a "worthless worker" or "no better than a beast?" Here we get to the nitty-gritty of the practice of humility.

> Humility asks us to accept the circumstances of life as they come to us. We mustn't think we're too good to do certain things. The goal is to be at peace within ourselves and to trust in God's help to see us through a difficult or unpleasant task. (Tomaine)

The fifth step of humility is that we do not conceal from the abbot or prioress any sinful thoughts entering our hearts, or any wrongs committed in secret, but rather confess them humbly. Concerning this, scripture exhorts us: "Make known your way to the Holy One and hope in God" (Ps. 37:5).[13]

CHAPTER 7. HUMILITY, 44–45

The sixth step of humility is that we are content with the lowest and most menial treatment, and regard ourselves as a poor and worthless worker in whatever task we are given,[14] saying with the prophet: "I am insignificant and ignorant, no better than a beast before you, yet I am with you always" (Ps. 73:22–23).[15]

CHAPTER 7. HUMILITY, 49–50

16 Step 7: "To recognize that I may not have the final answer and so to listen to other people" (Tomaine).

Ouch! We might want to skip over this step of humility, finding it distasteful and, of course, totally untrue, but let's take a look.

One of the main goals of Benedict's community is to strive for purity of heart by turning away from the eight powerful thoughts that undermine the search for God. See "Turning to God," note 47. This step of humility helps monastics move away from vanity and pride, qualities that build up the ego and lead each to think he or she is above the others.

17 Step 7 is also about recognizing sinfulness and shortcomings. It reminds members once again that all people are worthy of respect regardless of their prior station in life.

〜 This step of humility may strike a familiar chord within us we do not want to admit or acknowledge: we often compare ourselves to others and place ourselves in the category of knowing more and being more important. Step 7 reminds us to always be aware of our thoughts and turn from prideful thoughts that separate us from others and from God. We are to honor one another. Here is a thought that might help us with this step: "This is not the same as a low self-image. It is a deliberate and sustained effort to be rid of the persistent delusion that I am guiltless" (Casey).

The seventh step of humility is that we not only admit with our tongues but are also convinced in our hearts that we are inferior to all and of less value, humbling ourselves and saying with the prophet: "I am truly a worm, not even human, scorned and despised by all" (Ps. 22:7).[16] "I was exalted, then I was humbled and overwhelmed with confusion" (Ps. 88:16). And again, "It is a blessing that you have humbled me so that I can learn your commandments" (Ps. 119:71, 73).[17]

CHAPTER 7. HUMILITY, 51–54

18 Step 8: "To take no action except those endorsed by people who show wisdom and understanding" (Tomaine).

Humility makes it possible for us to learn from others and ask for advice and counsel. An old Jewish proverb reads, "It's better to ask the way ten times than to take the wrong road once" (Chittister), which is something a proud person could *never* do. But many of us today distrust authority; we do not honor tradition nor respect seniority. Independent initiative *can* lead to positive change. Perhaps an image from my church choir will help here. We need to sing the same anthem. We want to blend together even though our voices differ in pitch, strength, and quality. We do our best to listen to our neighbors and the whole choir so that we create a beautiful harmony. I think this is what Benedict was after in his view of community—harmony, not sameness.

The next three steps address the role of speech in humility. They encourage ways of communicating that promote peace, calm, and harmony. While we may not agree totally with their substance, these steps offer food for thought about our own speech.

19 Step 9: "To listen more than talk" (Tomaine).

Two quotes from scripture illustrate two negative aspects of excessive speech: saying things we regret later and wandering in a haze of self-absorption. Want a refresher on why we need to listen more than talk? See what else Benedict says about restraining speech in "Living with Integrity and Virtue," RB 6.1–8 and notes 38–42.

Today our talk is not only through speech. Our thoughts can be e-mailed, texted, or posted on social media. We spend countless hours sending our opinions aloft electronically. What might we be avoiding through verbal or electronic talk? Do we wander about in endless Internet chats? When sending people to small-group discussions, a friend of mine gives this advice: "Be lean on speech and long on listening."

The eighth step of humility is that we do only what is endorsed by the common rule of the monastery and the example set by the prioress or abbot.[18]

CHAPTER 7. HUMILITY, 55

The ninth step of humility is that we control our tongues and remain silent, not speaking unless asked a question,[19] for scripture warns, "In a flood of words you will not avoid sinning" (Prov. 10:19), and "A talkative person goes about aimlessly on earth" (Ps. 140:12).

CHAPTER 7. HUMILITY, 56–58

20 Step 10: "To not laugh excessively" (Tomaine).

We know that laughter has positive benefits for both mind and body. Are we not to laugh in Benedict's world? That Benedict addresses excessive laughter means that there indeed is laughter in the monastery. He is cautioning against the love of frivolity, not laughter itself. Both excessive talk and laughter are ways of drawing attention to oneself, which is contrary to humility.

Have you ever been around a person who was continually yukking it up? What was that like? Imagine this scenario when you are trying to pray. Laughter can also be harmful when others are the object of mirth.

21 Step 11: "To speak quietly and briefly with humility and restraint" (Tomaine).

While Step 9 is a caution against excessive speech, Step 11 describes the appropriate way to speak.

Okay, what quality in verses 60–61 would you like to sign up for? Some might consider a person who speaks like this to be boring but Benedictines strive to be who they are in God's eyes—loved but not needing to prove themselves better than others. Humility speaks with respect, restraint, and reserve. I think it is a wonderful model to follow.

The tenth step of humility is that we are not given to ready laughter,[20] for it is written: "Only fools raise their voices in laughter" (Sir. 21:23).

CHAPTER 7. HUMILITY, 59

The eleventh step of humility is that we speak gently and without laughter, seriously and with becoming modesty, briefly and reasonably, but without raising our voices,[21] as it is written: "The wise are known by few words."

CHAPTER 7. HUMILITY, 60–61

22 Step 12: "To know myself and my limitations, yet know I'm forever in God's presence and held in God's constant love; therefore I can live calmly and peacefully" (Tomaine).

Benedict presents a picture of who we are when we arrive at the twelfth step—humble both in actions and inner disposition of the heart. Without the latter, the former is impossible.

23 The traditional posture for humility in the monastic community of Benedict's day. In Benedict's world, monastics of humility recognize their sinfulness, how they miss the mark in their actions and thoughts.

〰 When we read verses 62–66 we may be inclined to opt out of humility. While today we do not take on everything in the Rule, nor do monastic communities, the essence of this step is worth noting: humility comes from within and brings a consistency of actions no matter where we are or who we are with. It comes from a realistic and honest view of who we are. While our eyes will not necessarily be downcast and our heads bowed, our hearts will be bowed before God and others in love, respect, and acceptance.

24 Here is the uplifting and hope-filled conclusion to the chapter on humility. The fruit of humility is love, God's love for us and our love of God that casts out all fear. Good actions flow from our love for Christ. Virtue is easy and natural.

Verses 67–70 link the growth of humility to action of the Trinity. This section is the only place in the Rule where all three persons of the Trinity are mentioned together.

〰 Are you ready to climb the steps of the ladder of humility? While I spend a good deal of time slipping off, I find that these steps pop into my awareness and, when I am mindful, help me be a person of peace instead of pomp.

The twelfth step of humility is that we always manifest humility in our bearing no less than in our hearts, so that it is evident at the Opus Dei, in the oratory, the monastery or the garden, on a journey or in the field, or anywhere else.[22] Whether sitting, walking, or standing, our heads must be bowed and our eyes cast down.[23] Judging ourselves always guilty on account of our sins, we should consider that we are already at the fearful judgment, and constantly say in our hearts what the publican in the Gospel said with downcast eyes: "I am a sinner, not worthy to look up to the heavens" (Luke 18:13). And with the prophet: "I am bowed down and humbled in every way" (Ps. 38: 7–9; Ps. 119:107).

CHAPTER 7. HUMILITY, 62–66

Now, therefore, after ascending all these steps of humility, we will quickly arrive at the "perfect love" of God which "casts out fear" (1 John 4:18). Through this love, all that we once performed with dread, we will now begin to observe without effort, as though naturally, from habit, no longer out of fear of hell, but out of love for Christ, good habit and delight in virtue. All this God will by the Holy Spirit graciously manifest in us now cleansed of vices and sins.[24]

CHAPTER 7. HUMILITY, 67–70

Humility in Other Parts of the Rule

〰️ While each example that follows reflects the first two steps (reverencing God and doing God's will), I note what other steps on the ladder of humility I think each illustrates.

25 We need humility to accept the differences in what is provided. With humility we know that what is given is based on need and not on either deprivation or favoritism. Step 3.

26 Benedict gives the criteria used by the abbot or prioress to change the rank of a member. Step 12.

27 Humility brings respect for the abbot or prioress and other members and their ideas. Step 7.

28 Being elated is the opposite of humility. Here "elated" means to be ecstatic about your achievements. Humility recognizes God's action. Step 1.

29 Pride and arrogance are the opposite of humility. Under their guise we lack a realistic view of ourselves relative to others and place ourselves above others. Steps 3, 4, and 6.

30 Artisans are not to be self-important because of what they contribute to the monastery. They should acknowledge that God gives them their skill. Steps 7 and 8.

Whoever needs less should thank God and not be distressed, but those who need more should feel humble because of their weakness, not self-important because of the kindness shown them. In this way all the members will be at peace.[25]

CHAPTER 34. DISTRIBUTION OF GOODS ACCORDING TO NEED, 3–5

Only in this are we distinguished in God's sight: if we are found better than others in good works and in humility.[26]

CHAPTER 2. QUALITIES OF THE ABBOT OR PRIORESS, 21

The community members, for their part, are to express their opinions with all humility, and not presume to defend their own views obstinately.[27]

CHAPTER 3. SUMMONING THE COMMUNITY FOR COUNSEL, 4

These people reverence God, and do not become elated over their good deeds; they judge it is God's strength, not their own, that brings about the good in them.[28]

PROLOGUE 29

"You must not be proud" (Titus 1:7). Shun arrogance.[29]

CHAPTER 4. THE TOOLS FOR GOOD WORKS, 34, 69

If there are artisans in the monastery, they are to practice their craft with all humility, but only with the permission of the prioress or the abbot.[30]

CHAPTER 57. THE ARTISANS OF THE MONASTERY, 1

31 Reading accompanies meals in Benedict's community with a monastic reading for a week at a time. See "Turning to God," RB 38.1–4 and notes 46–48. Monastics are also called upon to sing alone in parts of the Divine Office. Readers and singers are to be thankful for their skills but should also remember that God gave them these gifts. Both this passage and RB 57.1 above should encourage us to use our gifts with joy to the glory of God and in service of others. Steps 7 and 8.

32 Monks who become priests might think they are better than the others because of their ordination. Pride must be replaced with humility. Step 3. Today in denominations such as the Episcopal Church, women vowed to Benedictine life in monasteries can also be ordained.

33 Priests must follow the Rule in obedience to express humility. Steps 3, 4, 6, 7, 8, 9, and 12.

34 Here Benedict is speaking of the deans, who each are responsible for a group of ten monastics. Step 2.

⟿ Owning up to mistakes is part of humility. It is a way of admitting and being okay with the truth about ourselves. Step 7. See "Turning to God," RB 45.1–2 and notes 21–22.

⟿ As a final example, humility is also needed in prayer. Steps 3 and 12. See "Turning to God," RB 20.1–2 and note 39.

⟿ Humility in the Rule is challenging but important. Did Benedict get your attention? What steps could enhance your own practice of humility?

No monastics should presume to read or sing unless
they are able to benefit the hearers; let this be done with
humility, seriousness, and reverence, and at the bidding of
the prioress or abbot.[31]

CHAPTER 47. ANNOUNCING THE HOURS FOR THE OPUS DEI, 3–4

Any abbot of a male monastery who asks to have a priest or
deacon ordained should choose from his monks one worthy
to exercise the priesthood. The monk so ordained must be
on guard against conceit or pride, must not presume to do
anything except what the abbot commands him, and must
recognize that now he will have to subject himself all the
more to the discipline of the rule.[32]

CHAPTER 62. THE PRIESTS OF THE MONASTERY, 1–3

Otherwise, [the priest] must recognize that he is subject to
the discipline of the rule, and not make any exceptions for
himself, but rather give everyone an example of humility.[33]

CHAPTER 60. THE ADMISSION OF PRIESTS TO THE MONASTERY, 5

Then, so long as it is entrusted to more than one, no
individual will yield to pride.[34]

CHAPTER 65. THE PRIOR AND SUBPRIORESS OF THE MONASTERY, 13

The Prioress or Abbot of the Monastery

〰️ The Rule's chapter 2 covers responsibilities, accountability, and ways of interacting with monastery members.

1 The prioress or abbot makes Christ present to the community through words, actions, and meticulous adherence to the Rule. Therefore, obedience to the superior is obedience to Christ. The prioress and abbot are to act in a manner worthy of the office which they hold.

2 The main functions of the prioress and abbot are spiritual leader and teacher. Here "teach" refers to the practical guidance of the monastics as they learn to live in community, grow in the monastic life, and seek God. Benedict uses the image of leaven from the parables of Jesus (Matthew 13:33).

7 □ Embodying Christ

Benedictine Leadership

If you want to be a better manager, supervisor, parent, or volunteer leader, you have come to the right place. The Rule presents a model for leadership characterized by wisdom, compassion, fairness, practicality, and spiritual focus.

In this chapter we look at the leadership positions of the abbot or prioress of the monastery, the cellarer who distributes goods and food to the community, and the deans of the monastery. Goodness of life is perhaps the most important quality of any member of the monastery but especially for those in leadership positions and particularly for the abbot or prioress.

To be worthy of the task of governing a monastery, the prioress or abbot must always remember what the title signifies and act accordingly. They are believed to hold the place of Christ in the monastery.[1] Therefore, a prioress or abbot must never teach or decree or command anything that would deviate from God's instructions. On the contrary, everything they teach and command should, like the leaven of divine justice, permeate the minds of the community.[2]

CHAPTER 2. QUALITIES OF THE ABBOT OR PRIORESS, 1–2, 4–5

3 The warning to the superior regarding the community's obedience is made four times in this chapter.

4 The prioress or abbot is a shepherd to the community, an image for Jesus that is used elsewhere in the Rule (RB 2.7, 27.8).

5 Wow—strong words! The "sheep" receive a stern warning that they will be punished for refusing the care of their faithful shepherd, the representative of Christ, who leads their community. Who they really refuse is Christ.

6 The prioress and abbot are to teach through verbal instruction (RB 2.11–12). But more important to Benedict is that each become a reflection of Holy Scripture, "a living Bible, in which we can easily read what is to be done" (Böckmann). Benedict varies the type of instruction with the ability of the individual monastic to understand and respond. Benedict asks the prioress or abbot to *really know* each member of the community in order to discern how to best reach each one with life-giving words or illustrative actions. This takes astute powers of observation, selflessness, deep love, and patience.

Another translation of "dull" is "simpler" (Böckmann); those who may be slow to understand or learn but are respected by teaching in a way that they can comprehend. In a beautiful image, Benedict asks each leader to become "a living example." Would that all of us become this.

Let the prioress and abbot always remember that at the judgment of God, not only their teaching but also the community's obedience will come under scrutiny.[3]

CHAPTER 2. QUALITIES OF THE ABBOT OR PRIORESS, 6

Still, if they have faithfully shepherded a restive and disobedient flock, always striving to cure their unhealthy ways, it will be otherwise: the shepherd will be acquitted at God's judgment.[4] Then, like the prophet, they may say to God: "I have not hidden your justice in my heart; I have proclaimed your truth and your salvation" (Ps. 40:11) "but they spurned and rejected me" (Isa. 1:2; Ezek. 20:27). Then at last the sheep that have rebelled against their care will be punished by the overwhelming power of death.[5]

CHAPTER 2. QUALITIES OF THE ABBOT OR PRIORESS, 8–10

Furthermore, those who receive the name of prioress or abbot are to lead the community by a twofold teaching: they must point out to the monastics all that is good and holy more by example than by words, proposing God's commandments to a receptive community with words, but demonstrating God's instructions to the stubborn and the dull by a living example.[6]

CHAPTER 2. QUALITIES OF THE ABBOT OR PRIORESS, 11–12

7 The second emphatic warning to practice what you teach. Leadership is serious business and accountability is to God. Benedict uses scripture to emphasize how critical it is for the prioress and abbot to personally follow the Rule.

8 Favoritism breeds discontent among those who are not among the favored and disrupts harmony in the community. Here, loving another is not based on personal feelings but on worthiness.

It hardly needs mentioning that favoritism should be avoided in families, the workplace, and other communities. My parents were good examples of this, although they once gave my brother a doctor kit and me a nurse kit. More a sign of the times than favoritism, however.

Again, if they teach the community that something is not to be done, then neither must they do it, "lest after preaching to others, they themselves be found reprobate" (1 Cor. 9:27) and God someday call to them in their sin: "How is it that you repeat my just commands and mouth my covenant when you hate discipline and toss my words behind you?" (Ps. 50:16–17).[7]

CHAPTER 2. QUALITIES OF THE ABBOT OR PRIORESS, 13–14

The prioress or abbot should avoid all favoritism in the monastery. They are not to love one more than another unless they find someone better in good works and obedience.[8]

CHAPTER 2. QUALITIES OF THE ABBOT OR PRIORESS, 16–17

9 Slavery persisted into the sixth century. Monasteries admitted freed slaves but were careful not to admit runaway slaves whom neither Church nor state granted the right of asylum (Kardong). As we learned in this book's chapter "Cultivating Love," date of entry is the main way rank is determined within the community. See "Cultivating Love," RB 63.1 and note 1.

10 Here Benedict stresses fairness, equality before God, good works, and humility. Do we treat all people equally or do we rank people by their appearance, socioeconomic reality, and job? Justice demands that, like the prioress and abbot, we treat each person with respect and fairness.

11 Benedict is a caring abbot who wants his community members to progress on the path toward God and salvation. In the pattern of a good psychologist, he realizes that one approach will not work for all. Nor will one approach always work for the same person. Drawing on the example of the apostle Paul, verses 23–29 address varying teaching styles with the monastic's receptivity. "The whole person is to be educated: his will, his inclinations, and all his energies" (Böckmann). To accomplish this, the styles of teaching range from threatening to tenderness and patience to rebuke.

〜 When we are observant and in the moment we can also vary our approaches in teaching or leading to build people up (1 Thessalonians 5:11).

One born free is not to be given higher rank than one born a slave who becomes a monastic, except for some other good reason.[9] But the prioress and abbot are free, if they see fit, to change anyone's rank as justice demands. Ordinarily, all are to keep to their regular places, because "whether slave or free, we are all one in Christ" (Gal. 3:28; Eph. 6:8) and share equally in the service of the one God, for "God shows no partiality among persons" (Rom. 2:11). Only in this are we distinguished in God's sight: if we are found better than others in good works and in humility. Therefore, the prioress and abbot are to show equal love to everyone and apply the same discipline to all according to their merits.[10]

CHAPTER 2. QUALITIES OF THE ABBOT OR PRIORESS, 18–22

In their teachings, the prioress or abbot should always observe the apostle's recommendation in which it is said: "Use argument, appeal, reproof" (2 Tim. 4:2). This means that they must vary with circumstances, threatening and coaxing by turns, at times stern, at times devoted and tender. With the undisciplined and restless, they will use firm argument: with the obedient and docile and patient, they will appeal for greater virtue; but as for the negligent and disdainful, we charge the abbot or prioress to use reproof and rebuke.[11]

CHAPTER 2. QUALITIES OF THE ABBOT OR PRIORESS, 23–25

12 The prioress or abbot must act promptly to free members from the faults that hold them back and to prevent actions from becoming more deeply entrenched. Eli did not stop his two sons from taking the meat of animals brought for sacrifice and all three perished.

13 Ouch! We know that physical punishment was used in Benedict's day. But we also know that then and today the abbot or prioress truly desires that all available steps be taken to save the souls of the members. The superior is also responsible for community harmony. Discipline is needed if that harmony is disrupted.

14 Another translation for "demanding" is "wearisome." I get weary just reading about what is required of the prioress and abbot!

15 The Latin word *blandimentum*, translated here as "coaxing," means to caress as a way of winning someone over (Böckmann). Encouragement is given through the gentle behavior of a leader who has "a knowledge of hearts" (Holzherr) and the ability to heal them. This is the kind of leader I would like to be.

16 The abbot and prioress do not have easy jobs but neither do parents and other leaders. The main job of any leader is working with people. For the third time Benedict reminds the prioress and abbot of the need to vary their teaching to help each member amend faults, grow in goodness, and move closer to eternal life.

They should not gloss over the sins of those who err,
but cut them out while they can, as soon as they begin
to sprout, remembering the fate of Eli, priest of Shiloh
(1 Sam. 2:11–4:18).**12** For the upright and perceptive, the
first and second warnings should be verbal; but those who
are evil or stubborn, arrogant or disobedient, can be curbed
only by blows or some other physical punishment at the
first offense. It is written, "The fool cannot be corrected
with words" (Prov. 29:19), and again, "Strike your children
with a rod and you will free their souls from death"
(Prov. 23:14).**13**

CHAPTER 2. QUALITIES OF THE ABBOT OR PRIORESS, 26–29

The prioress and abbot must always remember what they
are and remember what they are called, aware that more
will be expected of one to whom more has been entrusted.
They must know what a difficult and demanding**14** burden
they have undertaken: directing souls and serving a variety
of temperaments, coaxing,**15** reproving and encouraging
them as appropriate. They must so accommodate and
adapt themselves to each one's character and intelligence
that they will not only keep the flock entrusted to their
care from dwindling, but will rejoice in the increase of a
good flock.**16**

CHAPTER 2. QUALITIES OF THE ABBOT OR PRIORESS, 30–32

17 Benedict uses "above all" to stress that the most important work of the abbot or prioress is the care of the souls in the community. "Absolute priority is the salvation of the souls, not good organization, not even discipline or any other monastic value. The precious nature of each individual person in view of his salvation is pointed out" (Böckmann). The prioress or abbot is not to focus on the administrative work of his or her position. People first—a priority that has eternal consequences for the superior.

18 The abbot and abbess or prioress are to put their relationship with God first and not be distracted by the things of the world, even if there is a lack of resources in the monastery.

More important words from Benedict: people are to be our first priority. I know that I can get consumed in the details of my work. These verses remind me that my true work is with and for people. And I am not to neglect my own spiritual well-being and relationship with God. We lack nothing when our hearts are focused on God.

Above all, they must not show too great a concern for
the fleeting and temporal things of this world; neglecting
or treating lightly the welfare of those entrusted to
them. Rather, they should keep in mind that they have
undertaken the care of souls for whom they must give an
account.[17] That they may not plead lack of resources as an
excuse, they are to remember what is written: "Seek first the
reign and justice of God, and all these things will be given
you as well" (Matt. 6:33), and again, "Those who reverence
the Holy One lack nothing" (Ps. 34:10).[18]

CHAPTER 2. QUALITIES OF THE ABBOT OR PRIORESS, 33–36

19 To make sure that they are completely aware of their accountability, Benedict closes with a final, somewhat scary reminder to the prioress and abbot—they are to be certain of their accountability to God for members as well as for their own soul.

20 Benedictine nun and scholar Aquinata Böckmann refers to Holy Scripture as the scaffolding for the Rule's chapter 2. Benedict continually turns to scripture for authority and direction. Böckmann also explains that within monastic communities today each member needs to possess qualities of the superior related in the Rule's chapter 2. I believe this applies to those of us outside the monastery as well. Here are the qualities she lists:

> Each is a father or mother to certain persons,
>
> Most in a sense are teachers, instructing and educating,
>
> Each is a shepherd responsible for certain groups and individuals,
>
> Each is accountable to the judgment of God,
>
> Each needs to place the spiritual over the material,
>
> Each needs to respect the basic equality of others yet also honor and adapt to their uniqueness. (Böckmann)

The prioress and abbot must know that anyone undertaking the charge of souls must be ready to account for them. Whatever the number of members they have in their care, let them realize that on judgment day they will surely have to submit a reckoning to God for all their souls—and indeed for their own as well. In this way, while always fearful of the future examination of the shepherd about the sheep entrusted to them and careful about the state of others' accounts, they become concerned also about their own, and while helping others to amend by their warnings, they achieve the amendment of their own faults.[19]

CHAPTER 2.[20] QUALITIES OF THE ABBOT OR PRIORESS, 37–40

〜 Scholars believe that the Rule's chapter 64, which is also devoted entirely to the prioress and abbot, was added later by Benedict under the influence of Augustine. Instead of grounding the instructions to the leader in warnings, Benedict centers them in love, concentrating more on the prioress or abbot as a servant to the community. The benefit to us is solid, Christ-centered ways to be a Christian leader and a person of Christ.

21 Because the abbot or prioress is so closely connected to members of the community, Benedict calls for a unanimous election and centers the choice in God.

22 The two key personal qualities for the abbot or prioress. As mentioned above, "teaching" refers to practical spiritual understanding.

23 Another use of "God forbid," showing the seriousness of conspiring to elect a prioress or abbot who would support the vices of a community and be lax in applying the Rule.

Should this happen, Benedict instructs bishops, any Benedictine leaders in the area, and other Christians to stop the election (RB 64.3–6).

24 The only mention of accountability to God in chapter 64. Without negative or threatening overtones, Benedict instead describes a leader who truly loves the members and wants to midwife their spiritual lives.

〜 I am struck by Benedict's use of the word "stewardship." To me it speaks to how the prioress and abbot use their God-given abilities to lead their communities.

In choosing an abbot or prioress, the guiding principle
should always be that the one placed in office be the
one selected either by the whole community acting
unanimously out of reverence for God, or by some part
of the community no matter how small, which possesses
sounder judgment.[21] Goodness of life and wisdom in
teaching must be the criteria for choosing the one to
be made abbot or prioress even if they are the last in
community rank.[22]

May God forbid that a whole community should
conspire to elect a prioress or abbot who goes along with
its own evil ways.[23]

CHAPTER 64. THE ELECTION OF A PRIORESS OR ABBOT, 1–2, 3

Once in office, the abbot and prioress must keep constantly
in mind the nature of the burden they have received, and
remember to whom they will have "to give an account of
their stewardship" (Luke 16:2).[24]

CHAPTER 64. THE ELECTION OF A PRIORESS OR ABBOT, 7

25 Following the example of Jesus, the abbot and prioress are servants to their communities. Pride has no part in this role, nor do self-serving, self-promoting actions. This is a countercultural way of leading for Benedict's day and, sadly, too often for our own. What if we decided to lead with this goal foremost in our mind? It would energize and inspire the people whom we lead, be it in the workplace, an organization, or even the family.

26 One way the superior brings profit to the members (RB 64.8) is through teaching Holy Scripture (divine law). In Benedict's day knowledge of scripture was not demonstrated by critical explanation of the text but by spiritual understanding gained through *lectio divina* (holy reading). This kind of knowledge brings monastics closer to God. See "Turning to God," note 33 and the unnumbered note "*Lectio divina* has been the mainstay ..." for an explanation of *lectio divina*. The old and the new could refer to the Bible as a whole, including both Old and New Testaments.

Let them recognize that the goal must be profit for the community members, not preeminence for themselves.[25]

CHAPTER 64. THE ELECTION OF A PRIORESS OR ABBOT, 8

They ought, therefore, to be learned in divine law, so that they have a treasury of knowledge from which they can "bring out what is new and what is old" (Matt. 13:52).[26]

CHAPTER 64. THE ELECTION OF A PRIORESS OR ABBOT, 9A

27　Benedict's treatment of discipline here has a humane touch not present in chapter 2 of the Rule. Deep compassion and love for the members are required. We are given the picture of a man or woman who leads yet walks alongside.

28　This is a favorite saying of Augustine.

29　This is a folk saying.

30　The abbot and prioress are to remember that they, too, can make mistakes and should exercise discernment in discipline. Benedict compares the prioress and abbot to the Suffering Servant of Isaiah (Isaiah 42:3), connecting them to Jesus, who refused to return evil for evil, and accepted crucifixion instead (Kardong).

31　Benedict uses the image of pruning, which in horticulture is done with care to promote the growth of the plant. Benedict's monks worked in the fields so this image would have been meaningful to them.

32　Benedict uses another quote from Augustine. To "strive to be loved" can be a great weakness in a superior if done out of personal hunger for affirmation. To prevent self-centered motivation, the goal for the prioress and abbot is to seek profit for the members and not honor for themselves (RB 64.8).

～　Verses 8–15 are filled with potential to help us be compassionate leaders. We would be wise to reflect on and strive to practice the actions and personal qualities encouraged by Benedict.

The abbot and prioress must be chaste, temperate and merciful, always letting "mercy triumph over judgment" (James 2:13) so that they too may win mercy.[27] They must hate faults but love the members.[28] When they must punish them, they should use prudence and avoid extremes; otherwise, by rubbing too hard to remove the rust, they may break the vessel.[29] They are to distrust their own frailty and remember "not to crush the bruised reed" (Isa. 42:3).[30] By this we do not mean that they should allow faults to flourish, but rather, as we have already said, they should prune them away with prudence and love as they see best for each individual.[31] Let them strive to be loved rather than feared.[32]

CHAPTER 64. THE ELECTION OF A PRIORESS OR ABBOT, 9B–15

33 These traits reveal a lack of humility, an absence of trust in God and an overabundance of self-focus. Benedict wants a prioress or abbot whose calmness can help build a peaceful environment. A superior who is never at rest will make that more difficult, if not impossible.

〜 There may be times when we are excitable, anxious, obstinate, or jealous, but we need not allow these traits to control our actions. We can develop the self-awareness to recognize these traits when they arise and "dash them against Christ" (RB 4.50). See "Opening Our Eyes to the Light from God," Prologue 28 and note 28, and "Living with Integrity and Virtue," RB 4.50 and note 24.

34 An alternative translation to "world" is "material matters" (Kardong).

35 Discretion has been named one of the key qualities of monastic leadership. Discretion—or discernment, as it is also translated—is a quality of avoiding extremes. The early Christian theologian John Cassian calls it "among the most outstanding gifts of the Holy Spirit." He sees it as "good sense" that is formed by wisdom, intelligence, and sound judgment (Cassian). Cassian encourages all monastics to follow the tradition of the elders and the goodness of their lives as a way to strengthen discernment (Cassian).

36 Once again, Benedict instructs the superior to be aware of the various temperaments and capabilities within the community and adjust expectations as appropriate.

〜 I appreciate Benedict's use of Genesis 33:13. When we are leading others and are filled with enthusiasm, this scripture verse helps us form reasonable expectations of others who may not be as energized.

Excitable, anxious, extreme, obstinate, jealous or overly
suspicious the prioress or abbot must not be. Such a person
is never at rest.[33]

CHAPTER 64. THE ELECTION OF A PRIORESS OR ABBOT, 16

Instead, they must show forethought and consideration in
their orders and whether the task they assign concerns God
or the world,[34] they should be discerning and moderate,
bearing in mind the discretion of holy Jacob, who said:
"If I drive my flocks too hard, they will all die in a single
day" (Gen. 33:13). Therefore, drawing on this and other
examples of discretion,[35] they must so arrange everything
that the strong have something to yearn for and the weak
nothing to run from.[36]

CHAPTER 64. THE ELECTION OF A PRIORESS OR ABBOT, 17–19

37   Benedict reminds the abbot and prioress to keep the Rule, but unlike the warnings in the Rule's chapter 2, the assumption here is that they *will* minister well. This is positive psychology: expect the best and the best will happen. Benedict again stresses that the superior is a servant.

〰   What did you discover in Benedict's chapter 64 that could help you become a better leader?

38   In addition to chapters 2 and 64, which are devoted solely to the prioress and abbot, Benedict provides further direction in other chapters of the Rule. In chapter 48 he instructs the prioress or abbot to be sensitive to individual capabilities. Contributing is important not only for the community and its needs but also for the individual who can then feel useful.

39   In monasteries all things are held in common. Personal possessions are given away upon entry. See "Seeking God," RB 58.24–25 and note 52. In chapter 55 Benedict explains that the abbot or prioress has the authority and responsibility to provide what is necessary for each monastic based on individual need. Distribution is to be done fairly without withholding what one member needs because others might be envious or jealous. Note the now familiar caution of accountability to God.

They must, above all, keep this rule in every detail, so that when they have ministered well they will hear from God what that good servant heard who gave the other members of the household grain at the proper time: "I tell you solemnly, God will put this one in charge of greater things" (Matt. 24:47).[37]

CHAPTER 64. THE ELECTION OF A PRIORESS OR ABBOT, 20–22

Those who are sick or weak should be given a type of work or craft that will keep them busy without overwhelming them or driving them away. The prioress or abbot must take their infirmities into account.[38]

CHAPTER 48. THE DAILY MANUAL LABOR, 24–25

In order that this vice of private ownership may be completely uprooted, the prioress or abbot is to provide all things necessary: that is, cowl, tunic, sandals, shoes, belt, knife, stylus, needle, handkerchief and writing tablets. In this way every excuse of lacking some necessity will be taken away.

The abbot and prioress, however, must always bear in mind what is said in the Acts of the Apostles: "Distribution was made as each had need" (Acts 4:35). In this way the prioress and abbot will take into account the weakness of the needy, not the evil will of the envious: yet in all their judgments they must bear in mind God's retribution.[39]

CHAPTER 55. CLOTHING AND FOOTWEAR, 18–19, 20–22

40 The cellarer distributes tools, food, and other items needed in the community.

41 The superior has the ultimate responsibility for insuring good care of the sick. Benedict uses "disciples" five times in the Rule, in chapters on obedience, restraining speech, and caring for the sick. "Brothers," translated in this inclusive language version as "monastics" or "members," appears over a hundred times.

42 In this book's chapter "Seeking God" we learned that the abbot or prioress calls the whole community together to seek input on important decisions. See "Seeking God," RB 3.1–6 and notes 27–30. Elders, discussed here, act as an advisory council to the abbot or prioress when the course of action on less important matters is not clear. Elders are monastics who possess maturity and wisdom but they need not be older in chronological years. Input could be sought by the superior on discipline or problems regarding material goods (Böckmann). Today, most important decisions are made jointly by the whole community.

∿ A year out of seminary and acting as the "newbie" sole priest in a parish, I sought the help of a supervisor. After sharing my carefully crafted plans for handling various situations in the parish, Bill often responded soberly, "If you do that you'll be sorry." We then discussed better options. "Do everything with counsel," Benedict teaches. How true!

43 If a gift is given, the abbot or prioress determines who receives it based on need. Today this instruction has been relaxed although personal gifts may still be given to others to meet a need. The prioress or abbot will also step in if it appears that a member is beginning to rely on outside support or income. The reason that Benedict cautions the member not to be upset is that envy, jealousy, and anger reinforce the strength of the ego and block the path to God.

44 Benedict cautions against presumption, a term he uses often in the Rule in connection with going against the prioress or abbot.

The abbot and prioress must take the greatest care
that cellarers[40] and those who serve the sick do not
neglect them for the shortcomings of disciples are their
responsibility.[41]

CHAPTER 36. THE SICK, 10

If less important business of the monastery is to be
transacted, the prioress and abbot shall take counsel with
the elders only, as it is written: "Do everything with counsel
and you will not be sorry afterward" (Sir. 32:24).[42]

CHAPTER 3. SUMMONING THE COMMUNITY FOR COUNSEL, 12–13

In no circumstance are monastics allowed, unless the
prioress or abbot says they may, to exchange letters,
blessed tokens or small gifts of any kind, with their parents
or anyone else, or with another monastic. They must not
presume to accept gifts sent them even by their parents
without previously telling the prioress or abbot. If the
prioress or abbot orders acceptance, they still have the
power to give the gift to whomever; and the one for whom
it was originally sent must not be distressed, "lest occasion
be given to the devil" (Eph. 4:27; 1 Tim. 5:14).[43] Whoever
presumes[44] to act otherwise will be subjected to the
discipline of the rule.

CHAPTER 54. LETTERS OR GIFTS, 1–5

45 The prioress or abbot delegates authority—to the deans, the cellarer, the porter who greets visitors to the monastery, and to the subprioress or prior. The prior (male monastery) and subprioress (female monastery) are second-in-command to the abbot or prioress. Notice the familiar criteria for selecting leaders in verse 4. Deans are to be humble and are given opportunities to change their demeanor if they show pride. The prioress or abbot removes deans and others from leadership positions when warranted (RB 21.5–6).

46 Note: "too often." As abbot, Benedict must have had difficulties with priors or observed the unfortunate consequences caused by priors or subprioresses in other monasteries, creating "envy, quarrels, slander, rivalry, factions and disorders of every kind" (RB 65.7). In the second sentence Benedict gives a few dangers of the lack of humility. Benedict recommends using only deans (RB 65.12) but allows for a prior or subprioress if the community asks for one—humbly of course (RB 65.14).

47 In spite of the strong caution against priors and subprioresses, Benedict offers a generous disciplinary process for a prior or subprioress who lacks humility or shows contempt for the Rule to make amends (RB 65.18–22). I include the last verse to show Benedict's caution to the prioress or abbot against taking action motivated by emotions.

[The deans] will take care of their groups of ten, managing all affairs according to the commandments of God and the orders of their prioress or abbot. Anyone selected as a dean should be the kind of person with whom the prioress or abbot can confidently share the burdens of office. They are to be chosen for virtuous living and wise teaching, not for their rank.[45]

CHAPTER 21. THE DEANS OF THE MONASTERY, 2–4

Too often in the past, the appointment of a subprioress or prior has been the source of serious contention in monasteries. Some, puffed up by the evil spirit of pride and thinking of themselves as a second prioress or abbot, usurp tyrannical power and foster contention and discord in their communities.

For the preservation of peace and love we have, therefore, judged it best for the abbot or prioress to make all decisions in the conduct of the monastery.[46] Yet the abbot or prioress should reflect that they must give God an account of all their judgments, lest the flames of jealousy or rivalry sear their soul.[47]

CHAPTER 65. THE PRIOR AND SUBPRIORESS OF THE MONASTERY, 1–2, 11, 22

The Cellarer of the Monastery

[~] All but three of the desired qualities of a cellarer listed in verses 1 and 2 impact relationships. Wisdom and goodness of life (maturity in conduct) come first, highlighting once again qualities Benedict sees as critical for monastic leadership.

48 John Cassian calls being greedy for food the chief root of other vices, to be eradicated by moderation (Cassian). As the person who distributes food to the community, the cellarer has plenty of opportunity to indulge in extra food and wine, and so must be a person who can keep these cravings in check.

49 The cellarer has a spiritual focus. "God-fearing" means "a selfless fear, a childlike reverence for God [that] causes the cellarer to see everything in the light of God and to do everything for the glory of God." Convinced of the presence of Christ, the cellarer discovers Christ in the least of the members and treats others so that they can recognize Christ in him or her (Huerre).

50 Where the superior is to be Christ to the community, the cellarer is to be like a parent. As a parent, the cellarer's words and actions are to be guided by love.

51 Although granted considerable authority, the cellarer shows obedience to the prioress or abbot.

As cellarer of the monastery, there should be chosen from the community someone who is wise, mature in conduct, temperate, not an excessive eater,[48] not proud, excitable, offensive, dilatory or wasteful, but God-fearing,[49] and like a parent to the whole community.[50]

CHAPTER 31. QUALIFICATIONS OF THE MONASTERY CELLARER, 1–2

The cellarer will take care of everything, but will do nothing without an order from the prioress or abbot. Let the cellarer keep to those orders.[51]

CHAPTER 31. QUALIFICATIONS OF THE MONASTERY CELLARER, 3–5

52 The cellarer cares for the goods of the monastery but more importantly for its members. The cellarer is not to treat the members in a perfunctory way, but lovingly from the heart. Cellarers are not to be disrespectful or use their power to mistreat others. An improper request by a member or one made in an arbitrary way is not to be met with a rebuke but with kindness. The cellarer is to be a model of love and respect. Another translation reads, "He should not put down the brothers" (Kardong).

〰️ Benedict reminds us that how we respond to others has consequences. When faced with unwarranted behavior or an inappropriate request, we are not to be judgmental or react to the emotions of the other person. By staying calm we can prevent an escalation in emotion and preserve love.

53 Benedict reminds the cellarer, as he does the prioress and abbot, that right and loving action impacts the soul. In Benedict's hands, the cellarer's work is transformed into a spiritual practice.

54 The cellarer is to show not just care but "*every* care and concern." The care is all-encompassing. Loving concern for the weak is one of Benedict's chief admonitions to the abbot, prioress, and officials (Böckmann).

The cellarer should not annoy the members. If anyone happens to make an unreasonable demand, the cellarer should not reject that person with disdain and cause distress, but reasonably and humbly deny the improper request.[52]

CHAPTER 31. QUALIFICATIONS OF THE MONASTERY CELLARER, 6–7

Let cellarers keep watch over their own souls, ever mindful of that saying of the apostle: "They who serve well secure a good standing for themselves" (1 Tim. 3:13).[53]

The cellarer must show every care and concern for the sick, young, guests, and the poor,[54] knowing for certain that they will be held accountable for all of them on the day of judgment.

55 As Benedict ensures that the sick, children, guests, and the poor are not neglected, he also instructs the same for the material goods of the monastery. Benedict reminds us that everything is holy and so everything is to be treated with reverence. "All things become bearers of Christ's presence.... Thus, everything is a priestly service, a liturgy" (Böckmann).

〰 Do we ever treat the tools of our work—the computer, hammer, or vacuum—as we would the chalice and paten for Holy Communion? Benedict asks us to look deeply at the things we use each day and to treat them with care. This is not just to keep things in good working order, which is important, but also to honor them as resources we draw upon to serve one another and bring Christ into the world. Using the tools of our work can become a prayer. When our work becomes a prayer we discover that the ordinary is sacred and our work is holy. Finding the sacred in the ordinary activities of daily life is an important Benedictine practice. Honoring our tools as well as our work helps us live as Benedict asks, "so that in all things God may be glorified" (RB 57.9).

56 Already in charge of resources, a cellarer might be tempted to take extra food and other items or give a greater amount than necessary to the members. Instead, the cellarer maintains moderation even when resources are abundant. Distribution of goods is guided by need, whether resources are scarce or abundant. We see a second reminder for obedience to the superior.

〰 When we have extra financial resources, are we more inclined to purchase extra things that we really do not need?

The cellarer will regard all utensils and goods of the monastery as sacred vessels of the altar, aware that nothing is to be neglected.[55]

CHAPTER 31. QUALIFICATIONS OF THE MONASTERY CELLARER, 10–11

Cellarers should not be prone to greed, not be wasteful and extravagant with the goods of the monastery, but should do everything with moderation and according to the order of the prioress or abbot.[56]

CHAPTER 31. QUALIFICATIONS OF THE MONASTERY CELLARER, 12

57　As parent to the community, the cellarer is to put respect and love for members first and do whatever is needed to promote peace in the monastery. Humility is the main quality that will allow this to happen.

58　The cellarer is not to get drawn into the emotion of the moment and act haughtily with a brother or sister whose request cannot be met. The Latin word translated here as "offer" also means "to stretch out," giving us a visual picture; the cellarer reaches out in love and understanding, offering a kind word to the person who is probably upset at not receiving what he or she wanted. Benedict understands the power of words to hurt or heal. Benedictine Abbot Denis Huerre gives this advice to the cellarer: "If he has to refuse a request, let him do it in such a manner that they depart joyfully, having understood that they are loved" (Huerre). In verses 13 and 14 Benedict illustrates the main job of the cellarer: to foster relationships based on respect and love as a model for the community.

〰️　Instead of treating people hurtfully, what if we remember these instructions to the cellarer and offer a kind word in reply? What if others made this a practice, too? We would all be peacemakers as Benedict asks in the Prologue to the Rule. See "Opening Our Eyes to the Light from God," Prologue 17 and note 17.

59　Verse 15 contains the fifth repetition of "all" or "everything." The cellarer is to take care of everyone and everything as directed by the prioress and abbot—a big job. However, the cellarer is not to claim or take over tasks delegated to other members even though he or she may feel more qualified. This is the third reminder of obedience to the prioress or abbot. Benedict is safeguarding the unity of the community and the authority of the prioress or abbot.

〰️　Have you ever jumped in and taken over a job that was given to someone else because you thought you could do the job quicker and better? I have. Next time, let's step back, respect the person doing the task, and be grateful that we do not have to add that job to our to-do list!

Above all, let the cellarer be humble.[57] If goods are not available to meet a request, the cellarer will offer a kind word in reply, for it is written: "A kind word is better than the best gift" (Sir. 18:17).[58]

CHAPTER 31. QUALIFICATIONS OF THE MONASTERY CELLARER, 13–14

Cellarers should take care of all that the prioress or abbot entrusts to them, and not presume to do what they have forbidden.[59]

CHAPTER 31. QUALIFICATIONS OF THE MONASTERY CELLARER, 15

60 Benedict again cautions the cellarer against misusing his or her authority and power. Prompt attention is a sign of mutual obedience and supports good relationships within the community. Prompt attention also makes grumbling by members unnecessary. "Led astray" is drawn from *scandalum*, the Greek word for a stone laid in someone's path to make them stumble and fall (Huerre). In this verse members are called *pusilli* (little ones); they have given away their possessions and freely become dependent, small, and more vulnerable—each one depends on the other (Huerre). With this in mind, haughtiness and lack of caring attention by the cellarer would cause hurt and anger. Jesus said if anyone puts a stumbling block "before one of these little ones who believe in me, it would be better for you if a great millstone were fastened around your neck and you were drowned in the depths of the sea" (Matthew 18:6).

61 Creating a calm environment is an important goal of the Rule. Things in the monastery are to be arranged so that no one becomes disquieted. Calmness helps the cellarer be present to Christ and to serve well. Benedict recognizes that to accomplish all this, help may be needed.

62 Just as there is a schedule for the Divine Office so that everyone knows what is expected throughout the day, so too for the distribution of goods. Such boundaries allow the cellarer to organize work and have time when goods are not being asked for and distributed. This is the third time in the chapter that "to be distressed" or "disquieted" is used as a condition to be avoided through good organization.

〜 This chapter in the Rule gives a tremendous model for each of us at work and at home. We can all be cellarers and distribute kindness, understanding, love, and respect to the people around us. And when we feel overwhelmed, we can ask for help.

They will provide the members their allotted amount of food without any pride or delay, lest they be led astray. For cellarers must remember what the scripture says that person deserves "who leads one of the little ones astray" (Matt. 18:6).[60]

CHAPTER 31. QUALIFICATIONS OF THE MONASTERY CELLARER, 16

If the community is rather large, the cellarer should be given helpers, so that with assistance it becomes possible to perform the duties of the office calmly.[61] Necessary items are to be requested and given at the proper times, so that no one may be disquieted or distressed in the house of God.[62]

CHAPTER 31. QUALIFICATIONS OF THE MONASTERY CELLARER, 17–19

The Evil of Grumbling

⟨∾⟩ Grumbling is one of Benedict's "pet peeves" (Kardong). He sees its impact on relationships and community; grumbling creates divisions and hard feelings between people as well as unhappiness for all, even for the grumbler. Whether audible or silent, murmuring turns the member from the goal of monastic life: the search for God and eternal life. Grumbling and prayer do not mix. Grumbling does not foster a meaningful life.

1 Monastics give up all personal property and so must look to the monastery to provide "all things necessary" (RB 55.18). Benedict knows that people grumble when basic needs of food, clothing, and other goods are not met. Meeting varying individual needs is an important practice in the Rule that has biblical roots (Acts 4:32–35). I do not believe that Benedict is using "weakness" as a negative characteristic, but to describe a person who may need more than others, perhaps because of a physical infirmities.

2 Once again Benedict uses "God forbid," so we need to take notice of what he wants never to happen—favoritism in the distribution of goods. Favoritism undermines trust and is just cause for grumbling. In verse 3 Benedict helps monastics learn how to respond in a positive manner to the way goods are distributed—they are to offer a prayer of gratitude to God. For the role of humility in acceptance, see "Choosing Truth," note 25.

3 Since negative feelings can arise when members see others receiving more, Benedict concludes with a classic admonition against grumbling. The sin for them and for us is that when we murmur we forget gratitude for what we do have.

8 □ Crafting a Meaningful Life

Moderation, Balance, Work, and Other Practices

In this chapter we will look at other instructions in the Rule that provide a holistic structure for life in the monastery, a framework that supports relationships, the environment, individual health, and the search for God.

It is written: "Distribution was made as each had need" (Acts 4:35).[1] By this we do not imply that there should be favoritism—God forbid—but rather consideration for weaknesses. Whoever needs less should thank God and not be distressed.[2]

First and foremost, there must be no word or sign of the evil of grumbling, no manifestation of it for any reason at all. If, however, anyone is caught grumbling, let them undergo more severe discipline.[3]

CHAPTER 34. DISTRIBUTION OF GOODS ACCORDING TO NEED, 1–3, 6–7

~ We sometimes grumble in our hearts or to others when someone gets something and we do not. My dear AT&T friend Peggy gave me an antidote years ago: "There's enough for everyone. It's just that someone may get something different from you. There's still plenty to go around." I think Benedict would like this idea.

~ Benedict also cautions against murmuring about others and the tasks that we are asked to do or must do. See "Living with Integrity and Virtue," RB 4.39–40 and note 18; and "Seeking God," RB 5.14–19 and notes 24–26.

4 This is the only place in the Rule where Benedict admits uneasiness in stating a requirement. Perhaps he knows that human needs vary and that it is difficult to hold all to a single norm. It could also be that Benedict does not want to micromanage everything with an endless list of regulations where the differing needs of individuals would result in all sorts of exceptions (Kardong). Wine was important because the water was often not drinkable. Even if Benedict's community was poor or experienced times of scarcity, a lesser quantity or quality of wine would have been available to them.

5 Coupling these two sentences together seems to show that the "infirmities of sick" may not refer to the physically sick but to those who psychologically want extra wine. In one of the earliest known commentaries on the Rule, a ninth-century abbot named Smaragdus writes that "the body is not able to observe abstinence outwardly unless the mind has given its interior consent to abstain" (Smaragdus). Scholars debate as to the size of this half bottle with some suggesting that it was equivalent to a quart (Böckmann). A standard wine bottle today is about three-quarters of a quart.

6 Benedict again suggests prayer: accept what life presents and give thanks for what you have. I wonder if Benedict wrote the last sentence with a firm hand, perhaps double-underlining the last three words.

"Everyone has personal gifts from God, one this and another that" (1 Cor. 7:7). It is, therefore, with some uneasiness that we specify the amount of food and drink for others.[4] However, with due regard for the infirmities of the sick, we believe that a half bottle of wine a day is sufficient for each. But those to whom God gives the strength to abstain must know that they will earn their own reward.[5]

However, where local circumstances dictate an amount much less than what is stipulated above, or even none at all, those who live there should bless God and not grumble. Above all else we admonish them to refrain from grumbling.[6]

CHAPTER 40. THE PROPER AMOUNT OF DRINK, 1–4, 8–9

7   The abbot or prioress creates conditions that make grumbling unnecessary. For example, they vary mealtimes with seasons and work, something not always done in the early monastic tradition where the hour for the one meal was retained at all costs.

8   Benedict expands the instruction to arrange *all* matters in ways to stave off murmuring. Benedict connects the spiritual life with grumbling, knowing that when people grumble they are not at peace and souls could be lost.

9   Another example of Benedict's understanding of human need. A hungry server is probably going to be uncomfortable, less than congenial, and prone to murmuring about the job and the members.

~   Does this mean I can nibble while I cook?

10   Although grumbling is not mentioned, Benedict's intention is the same as for the kitchen workers: readers are respected and cared for. Then there is then no need to murmur.

~   When are we expecting too much from others and from ourselves that could result in hardship and justifiable grumbling? How might we arrange tasks for ourselves and others to make grumbling unnecessary?

From Easter to Pentecost, the monastics eat at noon and take supper in the evening. Beginning with Pentecost and continuing throughout the summer, the members fast until midafternoon on Wednesday and Friday, unless they are working in the fields or the summer heat is oppressive. On the other days they eat dinner at noon. Indeed, the abbot or prioress may decide that they should continue to eat dinner at noon every day if they have work in the fields or if the summer heat remains extreme.[7] Similarly, they should so regulate and arrange all matters that souls may be saved and the members may go about their activities without justifiable grumbling.[8]

CHAPTER 41. THE TIMES FOR MEALS, 1–5

An hour before mealtime, the kitchen workers of the week should each receive a drink and some bread over and above the regular portion, so that at mealtime, they may serve one another without grumbling or hardship.[9]

CHAPTER 35. KITCHEN SERVERS OF THE WEEK, 12–13

Because of Communion and because the fast may be too hard for them to bear, the one who is reader for the week is to receive some diluted wine before beginning to read.[10]

CHAPTER 38. THE READER FOR THE WEEK, 10

Work and Balance

11 In the Rule, work is important as a way to use one's gifts and to serve others. While inheriting concern about idleness from the Desert Fathers and Mothers, Benedict has a more moderate approach toward work; he balances work with other activities of monastic life. In Benedict's time manual labor centered around garden, grounds, and monastery buildings. Benedict's members worked in the kitchen and garden; they tended animals and copied books. This is not busywork but work necessary for the life and sustenance of the community. Like their forebears, today's monastics work in garden, grounds, and monastery buildings. Monastics also manage the monastery's retreat house and gift shop and may work outside the monastery.

As he does for the Divine Office (RB chapters 8, 10, 15) and meals discussed above, Benedict begins the schedule with Easter, signaling its importance to the community and to Christian life. The Divine Office times vary according to the time of year. See "Turning to God," RB 8.4 and note 15.

For most of us the it is not idleness but busyness that is the enemy of the soul. We can heed Benedict's approach to work, including it among the many important activities while not making it the driving force of life. I appreciate that Benedict allows for rest, something I am always reluctant to do even though I have his permission. When visiting Italy I took note of the long midday meals common in that country. Did the practice originate in Benedictine monasteries where post-meal naps were allowed?

Idleness is the enemy of the soul. Therefore, the community members should have specified periods for manual labor as well as for prayerful reading. We believe that the times for both may be arranged as follows: From Easter to the first of October, they will spend their mornings after Prime till about the fourth hour at whatever work needs to be done. From the fourth hour until the time of Sext, they will devote themselves to reading. But after Sext and their meal, they may rest on their beds in complete silence; should any members wish to read privately, let them do so, but without disturbing the others. They should say None a little early, about midway through the eighth hour, and then until Vespers they are to return to whatever work is necessary.[11]

CHAPTER 48. THE DAILY MANUAL LABOR, 1–6

12 Benedict encourages members weighed down with tough work by having them identify with their spiritual forebears. He combines approval for hard work with an instruction for moderation, almost as if he were saying, "Work hard, but don't go overboard." Great advice for us today as well.

How do modern monasteries work toward a balanced life? Along with attending the Divine Office and Holy Eucharist, monastics have other responsibilities to the community and are busy people like us. Most monasteries today make and sell goods such as incense, candy, beer, wine, books, and other publications. Some run schools, colleges, and universities as well as active retreat houses. Benedictine scholar Terrence Kardong explains that a "common problem in modern monasteries of the Western world is overwork along with affluence.... The work, whether it be educational or industrial, becomes so demanding as to sap most of the energy of monks" (Kardong). Does our work become so demanding as to sap most of our energies?

Benedict's concern for the community is balanced by his compassion for individual capabilities. No one is to be idle, yet work is not to crush or discourage a person. Such defeat could put spiritual progress at risk. See "Embodying Christ," RB 48.24–25 and note 38.

Maybe you do not feel up to writing a proposal, cleaning the house, or mowing the lawn. Do a light task instead: tidy your desk, take the dishes out of the dishwasher, or clean out a small drawer. Be mindful of how you feel physically and mentally. Offer that same gift to people with whom you work or supervise and to your family. Following Benedict's instructions here is a sign of respect and love.

They must not become distressed if local conditions or their poverty should force them to do the harvesting themselves. When they live by the labor of their hands, as our ancestors and the apostles did, then they are really monastics. Yet, all things are to be done with moderation on account of the fainthearted.[12]

CHAPTER 48. THE DAILY MANUAL LABOR, 7–9

13 Benedict gives holy reading priority on Sundays. I wish that I could report that my Sundays are dedicated to reading (*lectio divina*), but after church they are generally consumed by errands, cleaning, and cooking, followed by a collapse in the evening—not very Benedictine.

14 Benedict is concerned for the individual as well for the community. Monastics who are studying or working may hold idlers in contempt, which will damage relationships in the community. Monastics who are idle need activity to prevent unproductive thoughts or actions that will undermine their search for God and their progress in the monastic life.

15 The Rule of Benedict 35.1–6 contains key aspects of work in the Rule. Work is done to serve one another in love. There is no hierarchy where one type of work is more important than another, nor is a person too important to do certain kinds of work such as kitchen service.

16 Notice that Benedict does not exempt nor exclude the weak from serving and receiving a heavenly reward; he provides assistance for them so the work can be done with a peaceful and joyful heart. Once again Benedict says that work is not to crush a person and help will be given when needed.

17 In a large community, exclusion from kitchen service is based on what is of greater benefit to the community.

18 "In today's society such service in love in the spirit of RB bears witness to a community free of discrimination where all members have equal dignity before God as a sign that all are Christian brothers/sisters" (Böckmann). Today most monasteries employ full-time professional cooks but the members are still needed to set up, serve, and clean up. I have seen both abbot and prioress disappear after dinner to return, with hair cap donned, pushing a cart ready to load with dirty dishes.

Verses 1–6 in chapter 35 are among my favorites. To me, the Rule is a guide to help us find ways to let love and charity flourish. I try to do kitchen service in love; I find this makes a big difference in how I approach the task.

On Sunday all are to be engaged in reading[13] except those who have been assigned various duties. If any are so remiss and indolent that they are unwilling or unable to study or to read, they are to be given some work in order that they may not be idle.[14]

CHAPTER 48. THE DAILY MANUAL LABOR, 22–23

The members should serve one another. Consequently, no members will be excused from kitchen service unless they are sick or engaged in some important business of the monastery, for such service increases reward and fosters love.[15] Let those who are not strong have help so that they may serve without distress, and let everyone receive help as the size of the community or local conditions warrant.[16] If the community is rather large, the cellarer should be excused from kitchen service, and, as we have said, those should also be excused who are engaged in important business.[17] Let all the rest serve one another in love.[18]

CHAPTER 35. KITCHEN SERVERS OF THE WEEK, 1–6

19 The Rule of Benedict 38.12 is also a favorite verse of mine. Benedict recognizes our need to be inspired by beauty and so instructs that we use our gifts, not for ourselves but for others.

20 The Rule encourages the use of God-given gifts in service of the community, but Benedict cautions against pride.

〰 We are to use our skills but not let them take over our lives. Our gifts belong to God. They are loaned to us to use and develop as best we can in service of others and with humility. Also, our work is not to define who we are.

〰 Benedict views the tools of the monastery with both spiritual and practical eyes. In the Rule, work is a holy endeavor offered using tools that enable the members to serve others. See "Embodying Christ," RB 31.10–11 and note 55.

21 The abbot or prioress keeps track of the tools and goods of the monastery (32.1–3), but here Benedict extends this responsibility to the whole community. Fourth-century theologian and monastic Basil of Caesarea writes that carelessness with tools is a sacrilege because these very tools exist for the service of God's servants and therefore they belong to God (Böckmann).

〰 Caring for the tools of our work is a wonderful way to recall the holiness of our service to others as well as a way to remember God's presence. Whether our work is inside or outside the home, before we begin and when we complete a task, let's give thanks for the tools we use.

Monastics will read and sing, not according to rank, but according to their ability to benefit their hearers.[19]

CHAPTER 38. THE READER FOR THE WEEK, 12

If one of them becomes puffed up by skillfulness in the craft, and feels that they are conferring something on the monastery, they are to be removed from practicing the craft and not allowed to resume it unless, after manifesting humility, they are so ordered by the prioress or abbot.[20]

CHAPTER 57. THE ARTISANS OF THE MONASTERY, 2–3

Whoever fails to keep the things belonging to the monastery clean or treats them carelessly should be reproved. If they do not amend, let them be subjected to the discipline of the rule.[21]

CHAPTER 32. THE TOOLS AND GOODS OF THE MONASTERY, 4–5

22 A lower price is often a way to undercut the competition. This is not Benedict's intent. Monasteries today offer what they make and sell at a fair price.

23 In an all-important phrase from scripture Benedict reminds the community that all work is holy and that "the purpose of a monastery is not to make money or even to survive economically. The business of a monastery is to glorify God" (Kardong).

〜 Regardless of how we are occupied on any given day, *our* business is to glorify God. "In all things God may be glorified" is for me the overarching characteristic of work in the Benedictine tradition. Whether we are working within or outside the home, for a salary or as a volunteer, whatever we do can be done to praise God; whatever we do can become a prayer.

〜 Have you ever been asked to do a task you considered impossible? Benedictine monk Terrence Kardong shares that ancient monks in Egypt were given "absurd and impossible tasks in order to break their self-will" (Kardong). This is not the case in the Benedictine monastery where the abbot or prioress uses discretion when assigning tasks so that "the strong have something to yearn for and the weak nothing to run from" (RB 64.19). In this spirit, Benedict instructs in chapter 68, "Assignment of Impossible Tasks," that after attempting to do a task members can explain to the superior why they feel they cannot do what was asked of them. We are invited to do the same when we find that we are overwhelmed by a task. For more on chapter 68, including the Rule text, see "Seeking God," RB 68.1–5 and notes 35–37 and the unnumbered note "Chapter 68 reminds us …"

〜 When I have been asked to do something that I felt was beyond my capabilities, I often discovered that, in the end, I *could* do what I considered an impossible task. The person who asked me had a better understanding of my capabilities than I did. Perhaps Benedict knows this as well.

The evil of avarice must have no part in establishing prices, which should, therefore, always be a little lower than people outside the monastery are able to set,[22] "so that in all things God may be glorified" (1 Peter 4:11).[23]

CHAPTER 57. THE ARTISANS OF THE MONASTERY, 7–9

Moderation

⟨∼⟩ Benedict emphasizes the need for moderation in all aspects of life.

24 Benedict again provides for the varying needs of individuals and work situations. Bread was the most important source of nutrition at the time. There is a question as to the actual weight of Benedict's pound, which would not equate to our pound.

25 Another example of flexibility in the Rule. "Provided it is appropriate" cautions for the use of moderation.

26 Benedict warns three times against overindulgence. I wonder if he had some unpleasant experiences with this in his community. Chapter 39 is the only chapter in the Rule that takes "every Christian" as the norm, which monastics are to exceed. Benedict quotes Jesus to drive home the point: Avoid overindulgence! See "Living with Integrity and Virtue," RB 4.36–38 and note 17.

⟨∼⟩ Right now I hear a container of something cold and chocolaty calling to me from the freezer. But fifth-century monastic writer John Cassian cautions, "the mind that is suffocated and weighed down by food cannot be guided by the governance of discretion…. Too much food of any kind makes it stagger and sway and robs it of every possibility of integrity and purity" (Cassian). Uh-oh—better memorize these Rule verses about overindulgence *fast*!

For the daily meals, whether at noon or in midafternoon, it is enough, we believe, to provide all the tables with two kinds of cooked food because of individual weaknesses. In this way, the person who may not be able to eat one kind of food may partake of the other. Two kinds of cooked food, therefore, should suffice for all, and if fruit or fresh vegetables are available, a third dish may also be added. A generous pound of bread is enough for a day whether for only one meal or for both dinner and supper.[24]

Should it happen that the work is heavier than usual, the abbot and prioress may decide—and they will have the authority—to grant something additional, provided that it is appropriate,[25] and that above all overindulgence is avoided, lest anyone experience indigestion. For nothing is so inconsistent with the life of any Christian as overindulgence. Our God says: "Take care that your hearts are not weighted down with overindulgence" (Luke 21:34).[26]

CHAPTER 39. THE PROPER AMOUNT OF FOOD, 1–4, 6–9

27 Chapter 37 of the Rule is beautiful, caring, and compassionate. The vulnerable among the community are given a snack before the regular mealtimes to help sustain them.

28 The estimated age here is seven to twelve. Children in the monastery eat more frequently so this instruction is not denying them anything. See RB 37.1–3 above.

29 Benedictines were vegetarians. Scholars question whether the monastics of Benedict's day even ate fish and fowl. They may have considered these too decadent. In the ancient world only the rich ate meat regularly. It was also thought that red meat aroused passions. Finally, bloodletting was used in the sixth century to heal sickness. Perhaps red meat was thought to replenish the blood.

As a vegetarian of twenty-five years I was delighted to discover this about Benedict's community. Their considerations, however, were different than twenty-first-century vegetarians. Meat is served in monasteries today, but individual monastics can opt for being vegetarian.

Although human nature itself is inclined to be compassionate toward the elderly and the young, the authority of the rule should also provide for them. Since their lack of strength must always be taken into account, they should certainly not be required to follow the strictness of the rule with regard to food, but should be treated with kindly consideration and allowed to eat before the regular hours.[27]

CHAPTER 37. THE ELDERLY AND THE YOUNG, 1–3

The young should not receive the same amount as their elders, but less, since in all matters frugality is the rule.[28] Let everyone, except the sick who are very weak, abstain entirely from eating the meat of four-footed animals.[29]

CHAPTER 39. THE PROPER AMOUNT OF FOOD, 10–11

30 More wine can be offered but, in the spirit of moderation, the prioress or abbot must be vigilant of overindulgence.

31 Reading these verses I cannot help but think that Benedict has a sense of humor or more likely a weary resignation about monastic life and his brothers, himself included (notice his use of "we"). Turning from the "unattainable noble goal [no wine] and the sad reality [monastics want their wine] he seeks a middle way and points to a realistic goal, a goal that he believes can be reached" (Böckmann). Benedict states this goal using scripture—a biblical plea for moderation.

~ Monasteries I have visited in the United States have wine only on major feast days and special occasions.

~ Discipline is to be done with moderation. See "Cultivating Love," RB 70.4–5, note 31, and unnumbered note "I like Benedict's use ..."

~ We encountered instructions for moderation in this book's chapter "Embodying Christ," for the abbot and prioress, RB 64.17–19 and notes 34–36, and for the cellarer in the distribution of goods, RB 31.12 and note 56. Benedict asks for moderation in speech for the monastics—and all of us. See "Living with Integrity and Virtue, "RB 4.51–54 and note 28. Moderation, with its partner, balance, can help us find open space to create a meaningful life.

The abbot or prioress will determine when local conditions, work or the summer heat indicates the need for a greater amount [of wine]. They must, in any case, take great care lest excess or drunkenness creep in.[30] We read that monastics should not drink wine at all, but since the monastics of our day cannot be convinced of this, let us at least agree to drink moderately, and not to the point of excess, for "wine makes even the wise go astray" (Sir. 19:2).[31]

CHAPTER 40. THE PROPER AMOUNT OF DRINK, 5–7

The Observance of Lent

〜 Benedict devotes an entire chapter to keeping a holy Lent in order to look forward to a joyous Easter.

32 Benedict sets the bar high but realizes that human nature is not likely to meet this goal.

33 Fasting has a long tradition in monasticism beginning with the Desert Fathers and Mothers, many of whom fasted to the extreme as a way of denying themselves for Christ.

34 The Lenten practice is to be an offering to God, not something done out of obligation.

35 Benedict's list of what a monastic might fast from is beyond food and drink. That Benedict includes idle jesting shows us that monasteries were not devoid of laughter. Also, Benedict does not say that *all* on the list must be removed but rather "some." Benedict's approach to Lent reveals the same moderation and realistic approach that marks the entire Rule. He closes this section by asking that joy be a part of the Lenten discipline. Christian piety has traditionally reserved joy for the Easter season.

36 While he trusts monastics to take responsibility for their Lenten practices, Benedict knows that pride about what one is doing can creep in. Prayerful permission can help keep pride in check as well as ensure that the Lenten discipline is not extreme, physically unwise, or dangerous.

〜 Benedict's expanded list of what we can give up for Lent beyond food and drink inspired me one year to give up anxiety for Lent. This resulted in a peaceful Lent and a heightened awareness for what triggers anxiety, which helped me to amend this fault ... somewhat.

The life of a monastic ought to be a continuous Lent. Since few, however, have the strength for this, we urge the entire community during these days of Lent to keep its manner of life most pure and to wash away in this holy season the negligences of other times.[32] This we can do in a fitting manner by refusing to indulge evil habits and by devoting ourselves to prayer with tears, to reading, to compunction of heart and self-denial. During these days, therefore, we will add to the usual measure of our service something by way of private prayer and abstinence from food or drink,[33] so that each of us will have something above the assigned measure to offer God of our own will with the joy of the Holy Spirit (1 Thess. 1:6).[34] In other words, let each one deny themselves some food, drink, sleep, needless talking and idle jesting, and look forward to holy Easter with joy and spiritual longing.[35]

All should, however, make known to the prioress or abbot what they intend to do, since it ought to be done with their prayer and approval. Whatever is undertaken without the permission of the prioress or abbot will be reckoned as presumption and vainglory, not deserving a reward. Therefore, everything must be done with their approval.[36]

CHAPTER 49. THE OBSERVANCE OF LENT, 1–7, 8–10

37 Benedict increases the time for reading during Lent. Monastics undoubtedly read Holy Scripture and perhaps also the Rule of Basil and the writings of John Cassian and the Church Fathers.

〜 That the Lenten book is to be read cover to cover hits home. I start books with good intentions but how many have I finished? Benedict asks for perseverance in staying with the commitment—a mark of stability.

Clothing, Sleeping Arrangements, and Other Practical Matters

〜 Have you noticed Benedict's care and concern for members of his community? Here he addresses clothing for the members—always practical, always in moderation—two characteristics we might also choose to adopt.

38 The prioress and abbot consider the comfort of members in clothing decisions. Benedict mentions the abbot or prioress seven times in this chapter alone, each in connection with a decision or task.

39 In Benedict's time monastic clothing was not considered a "habit," as we know it today. The cowl, which literally means "little house," was a large, loose outer garment with a hood. The tunic was a close-fitting garment usually worn next to the skin and was similar to the present-day cassock worn by priests and often choir members, although shorter, ending at the knees. The tunic was usually gathered at the waist (Kardong). Although we are not sure that this was the garment that Benedict intended, a scapular, worn over the tunic, was a long piece of black fabric that went over the head and was suspended front and back from the shoulders. Benedict does not mention color, but Benedictines traditionally wear black and Cistercians white. Perhaps this neutral approach has roots in ancient times when color was associated with luxury (Kardong).

40 Benedict includes this instruction because some of the members from noble or wealthy backgrounds were used to finer clothing than what monastics wear. While the clothing is not luxurious, it needs to fit.

During the days of Lent, they should be free in the morning to read until the third hour, after which they will work at their assigned tasks until the end of the tenth hour. During this time of Lent each one is to receive a book from the library and is to read the whole of it straight through. These books are to be distributed at the beginning of Lent.[37]

CHAPTER 48. THE DAILY MANUAL LABOR, 14–16

The clothing distributed to the members should vary according to local conditions and climate, because more is needed in cold regions and less in warmer. This is left to the discretion of the prioress or abbot.[38] We believe that for each monastic a cowl and tunic will suffice in temperate regions; in winter a woolen cowl is necessary, in summer a thinner or worn one; also a scapular for work, and footwear—both sandals and shoes.[39]

Monastics must not complain about the color or coarseness of all these articles, but use what is available in the vicinity at a reasonable cost. However, the prioress and abbot ought to be concerned about the measurements of these garments that they not be too short but fitted to the wearers.[40]

CHAPTER 55. CLOTHING AND FOOTWEAR, 1–6, 7–8

41 Twice Benedict instructs that old items are to be returned when new ones are received. Hiding back-up clothing just in case is not appropriate for members who are to look to the prioress or abbot for all their needs. Benedict says that the poor can use the clothing. This does not mean, however, that monastics are wealthy.

The provision of two garments was a very old one. Unlike us, monastics slept in the clothing that they wore during the day. They were not short of clothing compared with the ordinary people of the day, who may have owned only one garment (Kardong). When going on a journey, members were to receive a better tunic and also underwear, all of which would be washed and returned to the wardrobe when the journey was over (RB 55.13–14).

42 This seems sparse to us but Benedict actually provided for more comfort than many people had at that time.

〰 I often give away something when I buy something new, but this is not always my practice. Like me, do you ever keep old clothing as back-up clothing, just in case? The truth is, if Benedict looked in *my* closet he would ask me to make satisfaction and then tell me to quickly unburden myself of most of it!

Whenever new clothing is received, the old should be returned at once and stored in a wardrobe for the poor. To provide for laundering and night wear, every member will need two cowls and two tunics, but anything more must be taken away as superfluous. When new articles are received, the worn ones—sandals or anything old—must be returned.[41]

For bedding monastics will need a mat, a woolen blanket and a light covering as well as a pillow.[42]

CHAPTER 55. CLOTHING AND FOOTWEAR, 9–12, 15

43 In earlier monastic communities members had individual cells. In the Rule, all sleep together but each member has a separate bed (RB 22.1), again something that was not common in ancient times when most people slept in groups (Kardong). The bed was also raised up rather than being just a mat on the floor. A lamp most likely is there to make rising for Vigils easier.

44 Night dress being the same as what is worn during the day facilitates modesty and readiness for Vigils.

45 Kardong delightfully translates this as "hasten to beat one another to the work of God—of course, with all decorum and modesty" (Kardong). This seems an oxymoron and conjures up for me visions of serious-faced monks speed-walking in a "spiritual competition" (Kardong).

46 Here Benedict is speaking of members young in age, perhaps teenagers. When referring to monastics of shorter tenure Benedict uses the term "juniors." What a wise decision to keep the kids apart! This plan would have been helpful when my confirmation class did an overnight at St. John the Divine in New York City. Dawn came as a blessed gift.

47 I love this verse. Here it could be connected to the prior verse, with the elders encouraging sleepy teenagers to rise for Vigils. Or it could be that all monastics are to encourage one another. We can do the same.

If possible, all are to sleep in one place, but should the size of the community preclude this, they will sleep in groups of ten or twenty under the watchful care of elders. A lamp must be kept burning in the room until morning.[43]

They sleep clothed, and girded with belts or cords; but they should remove their knives, lest they accidentally cut themselves in their sleep. Thus the members will always be ready to arise without delay when the signal is given;[44] each will hasten to arrive at the Opus Dei before the others, yet with all dignity and decorum.[45]

The younger members should not have their beds next to each other, but interspersed among those of the elders.[46]

On arising for the Opus Dei, they will quietly encourage each other, for the sleepy like to make excuses.[47]

CHAPTER 22. THE SLEEPING ARRANGEMENTS OF MONASTICS, 3–4, 5–6, 7, 8

48   Benedict gives instructions here for the practical care of the sick. From the time of Pachomius it was customary for the sick to have a separate room, facilitating care and healing as well as preventing disruption to monastery life (Böckmann). Always primarily concerned about personal qualities, Benedict gives three important characteristics for those who serve the sick. The reverence of God is the foundation of all others. Attendants to the sick "must live in the presence of God, be led by the spirit of God, recognize Christ in every least one, and serve him" (Böckmann). For more on care of the sick see "Cultivating Love," RB 36.1–3, 4–6 and notes 38–40.

49   The early ascetics, such as Antony, renounced baths, which were often taken daily by Romans in public or private baths. Early Christians did not take baths for pleasure but for purity and health (Böckmann). Monastics might take baths two or three times a year. Benedict allows the sick to take frequent baths and seems not to legislate bathing to only a few times a year.

Monasteries today have rooms for the sick and even eldercare. Steps are taken to help these members still take part in community life. Wheelchairs, walkers, and even the use of technology help ill and elderly members be less isolated.

Let a separate room be designated for the sick, and let them be served by an attendant who is God-fearing, attentive and concerned.[48] The sick may take baths whenever it is advisable, but the healthy, and especially the young, should receive permission less readily.[49] Moreover, to regain their strength, the sick who are very weak may eat meat, but when their health improves, they should all abstain from meat as usual.

CHAPTER 36. THE SICK, 7–9

50 One final topic on practical matters—private ownership, a spiritual issue for Benedict. He covers this in a firm tone, likening private ownership to a weed. Having private possessions is an act of personal will instead of obedience. Also, everything belongs to the whole community, following the practice of the early Church as described in Acts (Acts 4:32–35). At the end of chapter 33, Benedict once again gives opportunities to amend actions before any discipline.

Benedictine scholar Aquinata Böckmann notes that this chapter "is one of the most important chapters for the realization of Benedictine life…. If a monastic should again grab things in order to have sole possession of them, the essence of monastic profession is jeopardized" (Böckmann). The essence of the profession is giving over oneself to the community, its leadership, and to Christ.

Throughout the Rule chapters are written in a way to highlight key points and this chapter is no exception. The structure used for this chapter on private ownership is illustrated below. Please find the words "nothing at all" at "D" below and in the Rule. To me, this is Benedict's main point and it is in the central idea of the chapter. Benedict surrounds this central point with a balanced presentation of supporting points as illustrated by the pairs of letters "A," "B," and "C," below and in the Rule. For example, the letter "A" shows that Benedict begins and ends this section with statements against private ownership. Take a few moments to study this structure below and in the Rule.

A. Private ownership: an evil to be uprooted.

  B. The prioress or abbot gives permission.

    C. Monastics are to have no possessions to receive or give.

      D. "Nothing at all"—the central idea of chapter 33.

    C. Monastics are to have no possessions, not a single item.

  B. The prioress or abbot gives permission.

A. Common ownership and not private ownership, is the monastic practice.

Above all, this evil practice (of private ownership)⁵⁰ must be uprooted and removed from the monastery.ᴬ We mean that without an order from the prioress or abbot,ᴮ no members may presume to give, receive or retain anything as their own,ᶜ nothing at allᴰ—not a book, writing tablets or stylus—in short not a single item, especially since monastics may not have the free disposal even of their own bodies and wills.ᶜ For their needs, they are to look to the prioress or abbot of the monastery, and are not allowed anything which the prioress or abbot has not given or permitted.ᴮ "All things should be the common possession of all, as it is written, so that no one presumes ownership of anything" (Acts 4:32).ᴬ

But if any members are caught indulging in this most evil practice, they should be warned a first and a second time. If they do not amend, let them be subjected to punishment.

CHAPTER 33. MONASTICS AND PRIVATE OWNERSHIP, 1–6, 7–8

〰️ Today there is less direct supervision by superiors and more responsibility on the part of the members. Discernment is required before asking for permission: "Is this necessary? Do I really need it? How does this fit into my relationship with Christ, with the community, into my solidarity with the poor? Permissions do not dispense us from the effort of discernment" (Böckmann). These are questions we need to ask ourselves before we add to our own personal property.

51 Benedict also addresses the consequences of private ownership in chapter 55. To uproot this weed, the prioress or abbot must provide *all* things necessary so there is no lack that could be a distraction or an excuse to conceal property.

The beds are to be inspected frequently by the prioress or abbot, lest private possessions be found there. Anyone discovered with anything not given by the prioress or abbot must be subjected to very severe punishment. In order that this vice of private ownership may be completely uprooted, the prioress or abbot is to provide all things necessary: that is, cowl, tunic, sandals, shoes, belt, knife, stylus, needle, handkerchief and writing tablets. In this way every excuse of lacking some necessity will be taken away.[51]

CHAPTER 55. CLOTHING AND FOOTWEAR, 16–19

1 The biblical basis for hospitality is receiving Christ in the stranger. Members of the community are also to *be* Christ to the guest and welcome all as did Christ. While Benedict would have accepted wandering monks such as gyrovagues as guests, he would not have received people who were not Christian. Today, monasteries welcome all people as guests.

~ If we draw nothing else from the Rule of Benedict, learning to welcome others as Christ (or as a child of God) will be a gift to all the people we meet. Benedict asks that strangers are to be received this way, yet the practice of welcoming others as Christ can also extend to family, friends, co-workers, people who serve us in places of business, and members of organizations to which we belong. "When we acknowledge the Christ in others, we acknowledge the part of them connected to God in Christ.... [You and I can] silently greet the Christ in the person" (Tomaine).

9 □ Welcoming as Christ

Benedictine Hospitality

Hospitality has a long history in the monastic movement, beginning with the Desert Fathers and Mothers in the early centuries of Christianity. When a guest appeared at a cell, the hermit ceased prayer and even broke a fast for the sake of extending hospitality to the stranger. Using imagery and vocabulary found in a monastic travelogue called *Historia monachorum in Aegypto* (History of the Egyptian Monks), Benedict gives his hospitality a distinctly desert monastic flavor (Kardong).

Benedict's instructions for hospitality are abundant and generous, but they also establish boundaries to protect the flow of life in the community. Both generous hospitality and protective boundaries are needed for us as well.

All guests who present themselves are to be welcomed as Christ,[1] who said: "I was a stranger and you welcomed me" (Matt. 25:35). Proper honor must be shown "to all, especially to those who share our faith" (Gal. 6:10) and to pilgrims.

CHAPTER 53. THE RECEPTION OF GUESTS, 1–2

2 When a guest is received, the whole community gathers because the guest is Christ! Another translation reads "hurry to meet them" (Kardong). All greet the guest joyfully in love. The community then prays with the guest. See "Turning to God," RB 53.4–5 and note 54.

〜 How do you approach strangers? With restraint? With curiosity? Tentatively with suspicion? Joyfully with curiosity? In the twenty-five years that John and I have been married we have always been a multiple-cat family, ranging from three up to ten. (Yikes!) It is fascinating to watch a new member to our feline cloister arrive into the mix. Observable are stares, cautious circlings, occasional paw swiping, lots of hissing, and frequent growling. Any of this sound similar to how we non-felines greet strangers? Our behavior may not be as apparent but we have our own way of staring, circling, swiping, hissing, and growling. Benedict provides us with a different model based on love of Christ and respect for all persons.

3 Fifth-century monk John Cassian writes of the monastic practice of prostration in prayer, when the Egyptian monastic would fall on the ground for a brief time during the Divine Office "as if only adoring the divine mercy" (Cassian). To lie face down on the ground is a universal sign of submission to a higher authority (Kardong). Here that authority is Christ within the guest.

〜 While I doubt any of us would throw ourselves on the floor before a stranger (or anyone else for that matter, unless the result of unsteady feet), we can prostrate ourselves in our heart as a sign of respect for the person and in recognition of Christ within that person.

Once guests have been announced, the prioress or abbot and the community are to meet them with all the courtesy of love.[2]

CHAPTER 53. THE RECEPTION OF GUESTS, 3

All humility should be shown in addressing a guest on arrival or departure. By a bow of the head or by a complete prostration of the body, Christ is to be adored and welcomed in them.[3]

CHAPTER 53. THE RECEPTION OF GUESTS, 6–7

4 The guest's visit begins with what is important to the community: prayer, scripture, and hospitality. The prayer most likely takes place in the oratory with the monastics. This is an act of deep hospitality, for "to pray with the monks is to penetrate to the very center of their life" (Kardong).

5 Benedict wants guests to understand that Holy Scripture guides the monastery. I think he also enjoyed an opportunity to educate.

〜 As a guest at Benedictine monasteries I have been accompanied by a member to the Divine Office, to meals, and to other community functions. Someone is always there to answer questions, ease the way, and help me feel a part of the community so that I can be fully present to the gifts that community offers. This mark of hospitality is a true gift. Let's be on the lookout for where we can provide the same in our lives.

6 John Cassian writes, "The requirements of the commandment demand that the work of love be carried out. And so I welcome Christ in you and must refresh him" (Cassian). Cassian's words are beautiful and inspiring. From the early days of monasticism, spiritual disciplines such as fasting and silence were broken to show hospitality to a stranger. As Benedict continues this tradition he also sets boundaries to protect the flow of life in the monastery. The focus of the monastic is to seek God, and so the spiritual disciplines that support this are preserved.

〜 The boundaries Benedict sets for hospitality encourage me to both offer generous hospitality and to know where my own boundaries need to be drawn.

After the guests have been received, they should be invited to pray; then the abbot or prioress or an appointed member will sit with them.[4] The divine law is read to all guests for their instruction, and after that every kindness is shown to them.[5]

CHAPTER 53. THE RECEPTION OF GUESTS, 8–9

The prioress or abbot may break their fast for the sake of a guest, unless it is a day of special fast which cannot be broken. The members, however, observe the usual fast.[6]

CHAPTER 53. THE RECEPTION OF GUESTS, 10–11

7 Benedict continues the ancient practice of foot washing, a sign of humility and servanthood. This action binds the community with the guest and honors the presence of Christ in the guest. Today foot washing is not the normal practice in the monastery.

8 This verse explains once again why guests are received with honor— the presence of Christ, which Benedict says is found especially in the poor and pilgrims.

9 Benedict carefully distinguishes between the words we translate as "fear" or "awe." *Timor* means "religious awe and wonder"; it is a word that Benedict uses frequently. The other Latin word *terror*, which is used in this verse and translated here as "awe," means "a natural fear of harmful things." While the rich are not to be feared as evil, wealth is not a motive for religious respect (Kardong). Benedict seems to caution against the power of the rich.

10 Once again, so as not to disturb the regular flow of life in the monastery, Benedict suggests a separate kitchen to serve the guests. I enjoy his comment about monasteries never being without guests and sense some weariness hiding behind those words. Today's monasteries are also rarely without guests.

The abbot or prioress shall pour water on the hands of the guest, and the abbot or prioress with the entire community shall wash their feet.[7] After washing they will recite this verse: "God, we have received your mercy in the midst of your temple" (Ps. 48:10).

CHAPTER 53. THE RECEPTION OF GUESTS, 12–14

Great care and concern are to be shown in receiving poor people and pilgrims, because in them more particularly Christ is received;[8] our very awe of the rich guarantees them special respect.[9]

CHAPTER 53. THE RECEPTION OF GUESTS, 15

The kitchen for the abbot and prioress and guests ought to be separate, so that guests—and monasteries are never without them—need not disturb the community when they present themselves at unpredictable hours.[10]

CHAPTER 53. THE RECEPTION OF GUESTS, 16

11 Benedict does not stipulate special skills for the regular kitchen servers who are assigned a week at a time. See "Crafting a Meaningful Life," RB 35.1 and note 15. However, in chapter 53 he requires monastics who are skilled in the kitchen and stipulates a longer assignment. Both requirements promote efficiency and organization and both support Benedict's desire that guests are well cared for. And perhaps both assure that guests also have tasty meals.

12 Benedict says it is okay to have help when it is needed. He wants to stave off grumbling before it has a reason to begin. We do not have to be overwhelmed and waste energy murmuring about it. While the prioress or abbot sends other members to assist, we need to ask for help. This is not always easy to do. Yet when we get help we are more likely to be happy to help others, as Benedict instructs here.

13 Here Benedict uses the word *timor* to indicate that the one entrusted with the guest quarters must fear (reverence) God. This is an important quality we have seen in other roles in the monastery such as the cellarer.

14 Always a thoughtful abbot, Benedict provides for the comfort of the guest.

15 "The house of God" could refer just to the guest quarters, although Benedict uses this term elsewhere to describe the whole monastery.

16 Wisdom is an important personal quality in Benedictine leadership. It is called for in the abbot or prioress (RB 64.2), the cellarer (RB 31.1), the deans (RB 21.4), and the members of the community (RB 7.61).

17 Here is another way that Benedict protects the flow of life in the monastery. Benedict seems not to want members to be distracted by chats with guests. Guests should not, however, be left with the impression that the monastery is unfriendly and unwelcoming, so Benedict asks members to explain the reason for their silence. Because guests are to be received as Christ, the monastics ask for a blessing.

Each year, two monastics who can do the work competently are to be assigned to this kitchen.[11] Additional help should be available when needed, so that they can perform this service without grumbling. On the other hand, when the work slackens, they are to go wherever other duties are assigned them. This consideration is not for them alone, but applies to all duties in the monastery; members are to be given help when it is needed, and whenever they are free, they work wherever they are assigned.[12]

CHAPTER 53. THE RECEPTION OF GUESTS, 17–20

The guest quarters are to be entrusted to a God-fearing member.[13] Adequate bedding should be available there.[14] The house of God[15] should be in the care of members who will manage it wisely.[16]

CHAPTER 53. THE RECEPTION OF GUESTS, 21–22

No monastics are to speak or associate with guests unless they are bidden; however, if the members meet or see guests, they are to greet them humbly, as we have said. They ask for a blessing and continue on their way, explaining that they are not allowed to speak.[17]

CHAPTER 53. THE RECEPTION OF GUESTS, 23–24

The Porter of the Monastery

⌇ There is no better model for hospitality than the porter, who serves as the first line of hospitality for guests who come to the monastery. Today many monasteries have guest houses with a guesthouse master who coordinates programs and visits by groups and individuals and sees that guests are welcomed and cared for.

18 Translations also read "a sensible old man" (Fry), or as someone once shared, "a wise old woman." Benedict asks for a person of wisdom and maturity who is not likely to get distracted; a person who stays put (stability), who listens (obedience).

19 An important characteristic of Benedictine hospitality is to be *available*. Guests never need wait. Benedict emphasizes this by using the word "always," which appears frequently in the Rule when Benedict wants to stress the importance of a particular action. Superiors of the monastery must *always* remember that they are accountable to God (RB 2.6); the monastic must *always* reverence God (RB 7.10); members must *always* be ready to arise from bed for the Divine Office (RB 22.6); absent members must *always* be remembered at the closing prayer (RB 67.2), and so forth.

⌇ There are days that my own availability score is pretty low; days when my head and my feet are not just roaming but rushing here, dashing there. A visitor to this chaos (friend, spouse, stranger) will not find me really present (stability) and available to respond (obedience). Perhaps remembering "a room near the entrance" will remind me to be more alert to a knock on the door of my life.

20   In ancient times the gates of monasteries were bolted at night, so a visitor needed to call for special help from the porter (Kardong). Notice that Benedict does not just say that everyone politely knocks at the door. In another translation of the Latin word *clamaverit*, a poor person "cries out," showing us an urgency perhaps from the pain of hunger or cold. Notice also that the porter does not keep the guest waiting but immediately responds to the knock or cry at the monastery door. The porter is to be *attentive*. Because the person knocking is to be welcomed as Christ, the porter expresses joy ("Thanks be to God") or asks for a blessing.

21   The porter answers quickly with two beautiful qualities: gentleness and the warmth of love. Notice that Benedict uses the word "all" in connection with gentleness. The gentleness and warmth of love are to be total. This way of being comes from the porter's relationship with God. As the porter reverences God so too can he or she reverence people. The porter is to be *accepting*.

⌇   In verses 1–4 of chapter 66 Benedict gives us a way to live with an open and loving heart. People come to us every day and "cry out." We can be *available, attentive,* and *accepting.* We can experience the joy of being a porter to them, a presence of *all* gentleness and the warmth of love.

22   The job of the porter is demanding and can be hectic in large monasteries. Benedict admits in the Rule's chapter 53 that monasteries are never without guests (RB 53.16). Benedict recognizes there may be occasions when the porter is overwhelmed with visitors. In order to treat each person with gentleness and the warmth of love, the porter may need help. A proponent of moderation, Benedict is against burnout on the job. The porter is not to be sacrificed for the guest.

⌇   Having been introduced to the role of the porter in the monastery, think about where you are a porter in your life. How might you be available, attentive, and accepting with all those God sends your way?

As soon as anyone knocks, or a poor person calls out, the porter will reply, "Thanks be to God" or "Your blessing, please;"[20] then, with all the gentleness that comes from reverence of God, provides a prompt answer with the warmth of love.[21]

CHAPTER 66. THE PORTER OF THE MONASTERY, 3–4

Let the porter be given one of the younger members if help is needed.[22]

CHAPTER 66. THE PORTER OF THE MONASTERY, 5

1 Why is this reason not covered at the beginning of the Rule in the Prologue? A possible explanation is that most of the Prologue was taken from the Rule of the Master while this chapter is Benedict's own creation, most likely added later in his life.

2 As we have seen before, Benedict is realistic in his instructions for moderation and balance. With a humility that is characteristic of this great abbot, Benedict considers that *both* he and his community will accomplish *only some* virtue and *just the beginnings* of what monastic life is all about. Monastic life here refers to the vow of *conversatio*. Monastic life and the life of a Christian are about becoming more and more like Christ in thought and action. Both are processes for a lifetime. "Virtue" does not mean much to us today. For Benedict it means "the movement of the whole person toward God in the power of the Holy Spirit" (Böckmann).

3 Desiring to inspire, Benedict now speaks directly to the more serious monastics who are eager for *conversatio*, the faithful living of the monastic life. This Rule is just a beginning and not the only resource. Benedict points first to those who aligned themselves with the orthodox position of the Church and whose writings were influential. Benedict himself turned to them for inspiration and guidance.

〜 Are you and I among the eager whom Benedict speaks to here or are we content with just *some* virtue and *just the beginnings* of a Christian life?

10 □ The Beginning of Perfection

Chapter 73 in the Rule

We have arrived at the conclusion of the Rule, chapter 73, "This Rule Only a Beginning of Perfection." Stated twice in this chapter, "perfection" means to make progress in the monastic life (Böckmann). The entire Rule is about this goal. What final words will Benedict have for his community and for us?

The reason we have written this rule[1] is that, by observing it in monasteries, we can show that we have some degree of virtue and the beginnings of monastic life.[2]

CHAPTER 73. THIS RULE ONLY A BEGINNING OF PERFECTION, 1

But for anyone hastening on to the perfection of monastic life, there are the teachings of the early church writers, the observance of which will lead them to the very heights of perfection.[3]

CHAPTER 73. THIS RULE ONLY A BEGINNING OF PERFECTION, 2

4 Benedict's enthusiasm in verses 3–4 is inspiring. Energy-filled words like *inspired*, *truest*, and *resoundingly* make me eager to explore Holy Scripture and the writings of the early Church all more deeply. Here Benedict aligns himself solidly with the orthodox Church.

5 Benedict now turns to revered monastic sources: John Cassian's *Conferences* and *Institutes*, the lives of monastic forebears, and the Rule of Basil. Other translations use "holy Father Basil" as a way that Benedict possibly united himself again with the Roman Church. "*Lives*" refers to well-known existing "biographies" of monks before Benedict. These writings serve two purposes: they are tools for progress in the monastic life and reminders of one's lack of zeal.

Members of Benedict's community are very familiar with work on the land. Transferred to their own lives, the image of cultivation gives a visual picture for their own spiritual practice. With tools (scripture and the writings) the soil (the person) is broken up, loosened, and made ready (obedience, the main element of monastic life) for the seed (of virtue and of Christ). The pounding rhythm of the closing words, seen especially in the Latin, seems to drive home the point that for Benedict and many of his community, they all have a long way to go.

The resources Benedict mentions are fascinating reading. In them I find plenty of food for thought and solid guidance for my own life. Human nature is the same today as it was several thousand years ago. We struggle with how much our personal will dictates how we live our lives. And we look for tools to help us live a meaningful and caring life.

What page, what passage of the inspired books of the Old and New Testaments is not the truest of guides for human life? What book of holy writers does not resoundingly summon us along the true way to reach the Creator?[4]

CHAPTER 73. THIS RULE ONLY A BEGINNING OF PERFECTION, 3–4

Then, besides the *Conferences* of the early church writers, their *Institutes* and their *Lives*, there is also the rule of Basil. For observant and obedient monastics, all these are nothing less than tools for the cultivation of virtues; but as for us, they make us blush for shame at being so slothful, so unobservant, so negligent.[5]

CHAPTER 73. THIS RULE ONLY A BEGINNING OF PERFECTION, 5–7

6 Benedict calls again to the zealous, echoing the urgency stated early in the Prologue: "Run while you have the light of life, that the darkness of death may not overtake you" (John 12:35 in Prologue 13).

7 Benedict has a job for his members—keep the little Rule for *beginners*. (It does not appear that way to me!) Benedict sees this Rule as a first step and in humility recognizes its small contribution. Christ will help on the way. Once the Rule is mastered there is more to learn and there are more virtues to acquire. Yet Benedict ends the Rule not with the challenging words mentioned above but with encouragement and a reminder that all things are possible with God who protects.

As a postscript to the Rule, I would like to share an observation about Benedict from noted scholar Aquinata Böckmann:

> We are impressed by his humility, shown by his awareness that he is always at the beginning, a sinner, a little one before the great God. Regarding his Rule, he also refers to the heights pointed out by others. He does not make his Rule an absolute. He is a man of liberty, opening himself and his monks to diverse movements within the church and in the world. He is a listener who knows how to choose the best. Above all, he is a person who always wants to advance, not alone, but rather together with his monks. (Böckmann)

And to those words I say, Amen!

Are you hastening toward your heavenly home?[6] Then with Christ's help, keep this little rule that we have written for beginners. After that, you can set out for the loftier summits of the teaching and virtues we mentioned above, and under God's protection you will reach them. Amen.[7]

CHAPTER 73. THIS RULE ONLY A BEGINNING OF PERFECTION, 8–9

Closing Thoughts □

You and I have journeyed together through this look at the Rule of Benedict. What do you think of the Rule? Remembering the very opening of
this book, do you *like* this Rule? What has struck you the most in the
Rule? What has troubled you? About what topic would you like to learn
more? What idea or practice did you learn about that could become a
part of your own "hastening on to your heavenly home"?

We are immersed in this process called life. Perhaps Benedict's Rule
will help us learn to live together with more understanding, to be more
compassionate, to listen more carefully to one another. With God's grace
and a heart "overflowing with the inexpressible delight of love" (Prologue 49), we can allow people to be our first priority, care more lovingly for ourselves and use our gifts with humility. Our life can become a
prayer to our Creator.

It has been wonderful to be with you. God bless.

Soli deo Gloria
To God alone, the glory

Notes ▢

Introduction

1. Esther de Waal, *Living with Contradiction: An Introduction to Benedictine Spirituality* (Harrisburg, PA: Morehouse Publishing, 1997), 41. Dr. de Waal, an Anglican laywoman, has written extensively on the Rule.

2. Esther de Waal, "Creation" in *The Oblate Life*, ed. Gervase Holdaway (Collegeville, MN: Liturgical Press, 2008), 205.

3. Joan Chittister, *Wisdom Distilled from the Daily: Living the Rule of St. Benedict Today* (San Francisco: HarperSanFrancisco, 1990), 4. Sr. Joan is a well-known writer and lecturer. She is a Benedictine sister in Erie, Pennsylvania.

4. Carolinne White, trans. and ed., *Early Christian Lives* (London: Penguin Books, 1998), xxviii.

5. Jane Tomaine, *St. Benedict's Toolbox: The Nuts and Bolts of Everyday Benedictine Living*, 10th anniv. rev. ed. (New York: Morehouse Publishing, 2015), 25.

6. Robert C. Gregg, trans., *Athanasius: The Life of Antony and the Letter to Marcellinus*, Classics of Western Spirituality (Mahwah, NJ: Paulist Press, 1980), 42.

7. Ibid., 7.

8. White, *Early Christian Lives*, xxxii.

9. Terrence G. Kardong, *Pillars of Community: Four Rules of Pre-Benedictine Monastic Life* (Collegeville, MN: Liturgical Press, 2010), 64.

10. White, *Early Christian Lives*, xx.

11. William Harmless, *Desert Christians: An Introduction to the Literature of Early Monasticism* (New York: Oxford University Press, 2004), 119. Adapted for inclusive language.

12. Ibid., 122.

13. Derwas J. Chitty, *The Desert a City: An Introduction to the Study of Egyptian and Palestinian Monasticism under the Christian Empire* (Crestwood, NY: St. Vladimir's Seminary Press, 1999), 24.

14. Harmless, *Desert Christians*, 125.

15. White, *Early Christian Lives*, xx.

16. Harmless, *Desert Christians*, 122.

17. Ernest Frederick Morison, *St. Basil and His Rule: A Study in Early Monasticism (1912)* (London: Oxford University Press, 1912), 4.

18. Ibid., 42–43.

19. Ibid., 102–4.

20. Timothy Fry, ed., *RB1980: The Rule of St. Benedict in Latin and English with Notes* (Collegeville, MN: Liturgical Press, 1981), 60–61. Fry is a Benedictine scholar who is a monk of St. Benedict's Abbey in Atchison, Kansas.

21. Ibid., 62.

22. Ibid., 63.

23. Ibid.

24. Adalbert de Vogüé, as cited in ibid., 64.

25. Kardong, *Pillars of Community*, 170.

26. John Cassian, *The Conferences*, trans. Boniface Ramsey (New York: Newman Press, 1997), 5–6.

27. John Cassian, *The Conferences*, trans. Colm Luibheid, Classics of Western Spirituality (Mahwah, NJ: Paulist Press, 1985), Conference 1, Section 5, 40.

28. Evagrius Ponticus, *The Praktikos and Chapters on Prayer*, trans. John Eudes Bamberger, Cistercian Studies Series 4 (Trappist, KY: Cistercian Publications, 1972), 16.

29. Luke Eberle, trans., *The Rule of the Master* (Kalamazoo, MI: Cistercian Publications, 1977), Chapter 13, 149.

30. Ibid., Chapter 50, 213.

31. Gregory the Great, "Life of Benedict" in White, *Early Christian Lives*, Prologue, 165.

32. Ibid., 165.

33. Ibid., Chapter 2, 168, 169.

34. Ibid., Chapter 3, 170.

35. Ibid., Chapter 8, 176.

36. Ibid.

37. Ibid., Chapter 8, 177.

38. Ibid., Chapter 8, 178.

39. Ibid., Chapter 33, 199.

40. Ibid.

41. Ibid., Chapter 34, 200.

42. Ibid., Chapter 35, 200–201.

43. Ibid., Chapter 37, 202–3.

44. Peter King, *Western Monasticism: A History of the Monastic Movement in the Latin Church* (Kalamazoo, MI: Cistercian Publications, 1999), 110.

45. Esther de Waal, *Seeking God: The Way of St. Benedict* (Collegeville, MN: Liturgical Press, 1984), 20.

46. King, *Western Monasticism,* 128, 130.

47. André Louf, *The Cistercian Way*, trans. Nivard Kinsella, Cistercian Studies Series 76 (Trappist, KY: Cistercian Publications, 1983), 37.

48. Ibid., 36.

49. Fry, *RB1980,* 133, 134.

50. Ibid., 135–36.

51. William Skudlarek, "The Monastic Expression of Interreligious Dialogue," *Benedictines* LXVIII, no. 2 (Fall/Winter 2015): 13. The Trappists are a branch of the Cistercian Order.

52. Michael Casey, "Monasticism: Present and Future: Part II," *American Benedictine Review* 65, no. 3 (September 2014): 311.

53. Jean Leclercq, *The Love of Learning and the Desire for God: A Study of Monastic Culture* (New York: Fordham University Press, 1982), 18.

54. Tomaine, *St. Benedict's Toolbox,* 30.

55. Fry, *RB1980,* 86. The holy catholic Fathers were influential leaders and orthodox theologians of the early Church and included Basil, Augustine of Hippo, and Gregory the Great.

56. Ibid., 90.

57. Ibid., 86.

58. Ibid.

59. Ibid., 90.

60. Tomaine, *St. Benedict's Toolbox,* 29. Modified.

61. de Waal, *Living,* 38.

62. Louf, *The Cistercian Way,* 33.

63. Ibid.

64. Fry, *RB1980,* 124.

65. Louf, *The Cistercian Way,* 33.

66. Ibid.

67. Ibid.

68. Elizabeth J. Canham, "A School for the Lord's Service," *Weavings* 9 (January–February 1994): 12.

Notes for chapters 1–10 are numbered to match the annotation in which the reference appears. Unnumbered annotation notes begin with the first several words of the quote.

Chapter 1: Opening Our Eyes to the Light from God

1. Aquinata Böckmann, *A Listening Community: A Commentary on the Prologue and Chapters 1–3 of Benedict's Rule*, ed. Marianne Burkhard, trans. Matilda Handl and Marianne Burkhard (Collegeville, MN: Liturgical Press, 2015), 6. Sr. Aquinata is a member of the Tutzing Missionary Benedictine Sisters in Germany and is a well-known and scholarly monastic writer.

9. Terrence G. Kardong, *Benedict's Rule: A Translation and Commentary* (Collegeville, MN: Liturgical Press, 1996), 9. Kardong, a priest, writer, and lecturer on monastic life, is a monk at Assumption Abbey in Richardton, North Dakota.

10. Böckmann, *A Listening Community*, 9.

10. Joan Chittister, *The Rule of St. Benedict: A Spirituality for the 21st Century* (New York: Crossroad Publishing, 2010), 7.

10. Ibid., 8.

11. Böckmann, *A Listening Community*, 23.

12. Kardong, *Benedict's Rule*, 558.

14. Böckmann, *A Listening Community*, 24.

17. Ibid., 33.

"In our personal universe …": Jane Tomaine, *St. Benedict's Toolbox: The Nuts and Bolts of Everyday Benedictine Living*, 10th anniv. rev. ed. (New York: Morehouse Publishing, 2015), 212.

19. Böckmann, *A Listening Community*, 37.

24. Kardong, *Benedict's Rule*, 16.

27. Böckmann, *A Listening Community*, 53.

27. Ibid., 54.

"Heaven is the state of being fully open …": Michael Casey, *The Road to Eternal Life: Reflections on the Prologue of Benedict's Rule* (Collegeville, MN: Liturgical Press, 2010), 150. Men and women in the Cistercian Order follow the Rule of Benedict and so are a part of the Benedictine monastic family. Casey, author of many books on the Rule, is a monk of Tarrawarra Abbey in Australia.

"If we wish to arrive at unending life …": Ibid., 153.

36. Kardong, *Benedict's Rule*, 31.

36. Ibid., 22.

Chapter 2: Turning to God

12. Terrence G. Kardong, *Benedict's Rule: A Translation and Commentary* (Collegeville, MN: Liturgical Press, 1996), 170.

17. Ibid., 199.

19. John Cassian, *The Conferences*, trans. Colm Luibheid, Classics of Western Spirituality (Mahwah, NJ: Paulist Press, 1985), Conference 10, Section 14, 139–140.

24. Teilhard de Chardin in Mel Ahlborn and Ken Arnold, eds., *Visio Divina: A Reader in Faith and Visual Arts* (Leeds, MA: LeaderResources for Episcopal Church and Visual Arts, 2009), 22.

"To love Christ is to love prayer…": André Louf, *The Cistercian Way*, trans. Nivard Kinsella, Cistercian Studies Series (Trappist, KY: Cistercian Publications, 1983), 111–12.

40. Jane Tomaine, *St. Benedict's Toolbox: The Nuts and Bolts of Everyday Benedictine Living*, 10th anniv. rev. ed. (New York: Morehouse Publishing, 2015), 97.

44. Kardong, *Benedict's Rule*, 299.

45. John Cassian, *The Conferences*, trans. Boniface Ramsey (New York: Newman Press, 1997), Conference 10, Section 2, 379.

54. Kardong, *Benedict's Rule*, 424.

"Gracious and holy Father…": Michael Counsell, comp., *2000 Years of Prayer* (Harrisburg, PA: Morehouse Publishing, 1999), 35.

Chapter 3: Seeking God

4. Adalbert de Vogüé in Aquinata Böckmann, *A Listening Community: A Commentary on the Prologue and Chapters 1–3 of Benedict's Rule*, ed. Marianne Burkhard, trans. Matilda Handl and Marianne Burkhard (Collegeville, MN: Liturgical Press, 2015), 103.

4. Böckmann, *A Listening Community*, 105.

7. Terrence G. Kardong, *Benedict's Rule: A Translation and Commentary* (Collegeville, MN: Liturgical Press, 1996), 40.

16. Ibid., 513.

19. Jane Tomaine, *St. Benedict's Toolbox: The Nuts and Bolts of Everyday Benedictine Living*, 10th anniv. rev. ed. (New York: Morehouse Publishing, 2015), 78.

31. Kardong, *Benedict's Rule*, 73.

38. Timothy Fry, ed., *RB1980: The Rule of St. Benedict in Latin and English with Notes* (Collegeville, MN: Liturgical Press, 1981), 459.

44. John Cassian, *The Institutes*, trans. Boniface Ramsey (Mahwah, NJ: Newman Press of the Paulist Press, 2000), Book 4, Section 3, 79.

45. Kardong, *Benedict's Rule*, 467.

55. Ibid., 560.

Chapter 4: Cultivating Love

4. Terrence G. Kardong, *Benedict's Rule: A Translation and Commentary* (Collegeville, MN: Liturgical Press, 1996), 518.

"Most monastic communities ...": Ibid., 525.

"There are few social problems more dangerous ...": Ibid., 573.

14. Timothy Fry, ed., *RB1980: The Rule of St. Benedict in Latin and English with Notes* (Collegeville, MN: Liturgical Press, 1981), 274.

14. Maribel Dietz, *Wandering Monks, Virgins, and Pilgrims: Ascetic Travel in the Mediterranean World, A.D. 300–800* (University Park, PA: The Pennsylvania State University Press, 2003), 108.

14. Ibid., 152.

14. Ibid., 120–121.

16. Kardong, *Benedict's Rule*, 501.

20. Fry, *RB1980*, 435.

"the healing code" Aquinata Böckmann in Edith Bogue, "Are There 'Hard Sayings' in St. Benedict's Rule?" *Benedictines* LXIX:2 (Fall/Winter 2016): 17.

23. Ibid., 222.

35. Kardong, *Benedict's Rule*, 358.

37. Ibid., 360.

40. Anselmo Lentini in Aquinata Böckmann, *Around the Monastic Table: Growing in Mutual Service and Love*, ed. Marianne Burkhard, trans. Matilda Handl and Marianne Burkhard (Collegeville, MN: Liturgical Press, 2009), 168.

41. Adalbert de Vogüé in Böckmann, *Around the Monastic Table*, 167.

44. Kardong, *Benedict's Rule*, 587.

45. Fry, *RB1980*, 293.

48. Kardong, *Benedict's Rule*, 592.

49. Ibid., 588.

49. Ibid., 593.

50. Ibid., 589.

51. Ibid., 596.

Chapter 5: Living with Integrity and Virtue

"Lists of tools such as Benedict's ...": Terrence G. Kardong, *Benedict's Rule: A Translation and Commentary* (Collegeville, MN: Liturgical Press, 1996), 82.

"Overwhelmed, most of us are inclined ...": Michael Casey, *Seventy-Four Tools for Good Living: Reflections on the Fourth Chapter of Benedict's Rule* (Collegeville, MN: Liturgical Press, 2014), xvii–xviii.

8. John Cassian, *The Institutes* trans. Boniface Ramsey (New York: Newman Press of the Paulist Press, 2000), Book 10, Section 22, 233.

10. Kardong, *Benedict's Rule*, 80.

14. Casey, *Seventy-Four Tools for Good Living*, 94.

14. Ibid., 95.

18. Kardong, *Benedict's Rule*, 87.

21. Casey, *Seventy-Four Tools for Good Living*, 156.

26. Ibid., 179.

27. Kardong, *Benedict's Rule*, 81.

31. Casey, *Seventy-Four Tools for Good Living*, 219.

37. Joan Chittister, *Wisdom Distilled from the Daily: Living the Rule of Benedict Today* (San Francisco: HarperSanFrancisco, 1991), 162.

41. Kardong, *Benedict's Rule*, 123.

42. Timothy Fry, ed., *RB1980: The Rule St. Benedict in Latin and English with Notes* (Collegeville, MN: Liturgical Press, 1981), 191.

42. Kardong, *Benedict's Rule*, 119.

Chapter 6: Choosing Truth

"And so, my children ...": *Historia Monachorum in Aegypta*, in Norman Russell, trans., *The Lives of the Desert Fathers* (Collegeville, MN: Liturgical Press for Cistercian Publications, 1980), 59.

"The Rule of Benedict spends only three paragraphs ..." Joan D. Chittister, *Twelve Steps to Inner Freedom: Humility Revisited* (Erie, PA: Benetvision, 2003), 53.

1. Michael Casey, *A Guide to Living in the Truth: Saint Benedict's Teaching on Humility* (Liguori, MO: Liguori/Triumph, 2001), 23.

4. Terrence G. Kardong, *Benedict's Rule: A Translation and Commentary* (Collegeville, MN: Liturgical Press, 1996), 137.

5. Jane Tomaine, *St. Benedict's Toolbox: The Nuts and Bolts of Everyday Benedictine Living*, 10th anniv. rev. ed. (New York: Morehouse Publishing, 2015), 214.

8. Kardong, *Benedict's Rule*, 141.

"We need to do battle ...": Casey, *A Guide to Living in the Truth*, 77.

9. Tomaine, *St. Benedict's Toolbox*, 214.

9. Basil of Caesarea in Kardong, *Benedict's Rule,* 146.

10. Tomaine, *St. Benedict's Toolbox*, 215.

11. Ibid.

13. Ibid., 216.

13. Casey, *A Guide to Living in the Truth,* 130.

14. Tomaine, *St. Benedict's Toolbox*, 216.

15. Ibid.

16. Ibid.

"This is not the same as a low self-image ...": Casey, *A Guide to Living in the Truth,* 150.

18. Tomaine, *St. Benedict's Toolbox*, 217.

"It's better to ask the way ...": Chittister, *Twelve Steps to Inner Freedom,* 58.

19. Tomaine, *St. Benedict's Toolbox*, 217.

20. Ibid.

21. Ibid., 218.

22. Ibid.

Chapter 7: Embodying Christ

6. Aquinata Böckmann, *A Listening Community: A Commentary on the Prologue and Chapters 1–3 of Benedict's Rule*, ed. Marianne Burkhard, trans. Matilda Handl and Marianne Burkhard (Collegeville, MN: Liturgical Press, 2015), 137.

6. Ibid., 138.

9. Terrence G. Kardong, *Benedict's Rule: A Translation and Commentary* (Collegeville, MN: Liturgical Press, 1996), 55.

11. Böckmann, *A Listening Community,* 147.

15. Ibid., 157.

15. George Holzherr in Ibid.

17. Ibid., 159.

20. Ibid., 165.

30. Kardong, *Benedict's Rule,* 534.

34. Ibid., 535.

35. John Cassian, *The Conferences*, trans. Colm Luibheid, Classics of Western Spirituality (Mahwah, NJ: Paulist Press, 1985), Conference 2, Sections 1 and 4, 60, 63.

35. Ibid., Conference 2, Section 11, 70.

42. Böckmann, *A Listening Community*, 199.

48. John Cassian, *The Institutes*, trans. Boniface Ramsey (Mahwah, NJ: Newman Press of the Paulist Press, 2000), Book 5, Section 20, 129–130.

49. Denis Huerre in Aquinata Böckmann, "Qualifications of the Monastery Cellarer—(RB 31): Part I," trans. Matilda Handl, *American Benedictine Review* 57, no. 1 (March 2006): 30.

52. Kardong, *Benedict's Rule*, 258.

54. Aquinata Böckmann, "Qualifications of the Monastery Cellarer—(RB 31): Part II," trans. Matilda Handl, *American Benedictine Review* 57, no. 2 (June 2006): 187.

55. Böckmann, "Qualifications of the Monastery Cellarer—(RB 31): Part II": 191.

58. Denis Huerre in Böckmann, "Qualifications of the Monastery Cellarer—(RB 31): Part II": 198.

60. Ibid., 201.

60. Ibid., 202.

Chapter 8: Crafting a Meaningful Life

"pet peeves …": Terrence G. Kardong, *Benedict's Rule: A Translation and Commentary* (Collegeville, MN: Liturgical Press, 1996), 332.

4. Ibid., 328.

5. Smaragdus of Saint-Mihiel, *Commentary on the Rule of Saint Benedict*, trans. David Barry (Kalamazoo, MI: Cistercian Publications, 2007), 411. The ninth-century abbot Smaragdus wrote the first full commentary on the Rule of Benedict.

5. Aquinata Böckmann, *Around the Monastic Table: Growing in Mutual Service and Love*, ed. Marianne Burkhard, trans. Matilda Handl and Marianne Burkhard (Collegeville, MN: Liturgical Press, 2009), 240.

"common problem in modern monasteries …": Kardong, *Benedict's Rule*, 388.

18. Böckmann, *Around the Monastic Table*, 116.

21. Aquinata Böckmann, "Qualifications of the Monastery Cellarer—(RB 31): Part II," trans. Matilda Handl, *American Benedictine Review* 57, no. 2 (June 2006): 190.

23. Kardong, *Benedict's Rule*, 461.

"absurd and impossible tasks …": Ibid., 567.

"the mind that is suffocated …": John Cassian, *The Institutes*, trans. Boniface Ramsey (Mahwah, NJ: Newman Press of the Paulist Press, 2000), Book 5, Section 6, 120.

31. Böckmann, *Around the Monastic Table*, 243.

39. Kardong, *Benedict's Rule*, 443.

39. Ibid., 444.
41. Ibid., 446.
43. Ibid., 224.
45. Ibid.
45. Ibid., 227.
48. Böckmann, *Around the Monastic Table*, 155.
48. Ibid., 157.
49. Ibid., 160.
50. Ibid., 59, 68.
"Is this necessary? …": Ibid., 67.

Chapter 9: Welcoming as Christ

Using imagery and vocabulary … : Terrence G. Kardong, *Benedict's Rule: A Translation and Commentary* (Collegeville, MN: Liturgical Press, 1996), 432. Kardong believes that this ancient source is the primary literary influence for this chapter, whether directly or through the Rule of the Master.

"When we acknowledge the Christ in others …": Jane Tomaine, *St. Benedict's Toolbox: The Nuts and Bolts of Everyday Benedictine Living*, 10th anniv. rev. ed. (New York: Morehouse Publishing, 2015), 146.

2. Kardong, *Benedict's Rule*, 423. Kardong feels that this translation is more in the spirit of the text, given the community is meeting Christ.
3. John Cassian, *The Institutes*, trans. Boniface Ramsey (Mahwah, NJ: Newman Press of the Paulist Press, 2000), Book 2, Section 7, 41.
3. Kardong, *Benedict's Rule*, 362.
4. Ibid., 425.
6. Cassian, *The Institutes*, Book 5, Section 24, 133.
9. Kardong, *Benedict's Rule*, 428.
18. Timothy Fry, ed. *RB1980: The Rule of St. Benedict in English* (Collegeville, MN: Liturgical Press, 1982), 287.
20. Kardong, *Benedict's Rule*, 557.

Chapter 10: The Beginning of Perfection

"perfection" means … : Aquinata Böckmann, *Perspectives on the Rule of Saint Benedict: Expanding Our Heart in Christ*, ed. Marianne Burkhard, trans. Matilda Handl and Marianne Burkhard (Collegeville, MN: Liturgical Press, 2005), 82.

2. Ibid., 89.
"We are impressed …": Ibid., 97.

Suggestions for Further Reading

Casey, Michael. *The Road to Eternal Life: Reflections on the Prologue of Benedict's Rule*. Collegeville, MN: Liturgical Press, 2010.

———. *Seventy-Four Tools for Good Living: Reflections on the Fourth Chapter of Benedict's Rule*. Collegeville, MN: Liturgical Press, 2014.

Chittister, Joan. *The Rule of Benedict: A Spirituality for the 21st Century*. New York: Crossroad, 2010.

———. *Wisdom Distilled from the Daily: Living the Rule of Benedict Today*. San Francisco: HarperSanFrancisco, 1991.

de Waal, Esther. *Living with Contradiction: An Introduction to Benedictine Spirituality*. Harrisburg, PA: Morehouse Publishing, 1997.

———. *Seeking God: The Way of St. Benedict*. Collegeville, MN: Liturgical Press, 1984; reprinted 2001.

Fry, Timothy, ed. *RB 1980: The Rule of St. Benedict in English*. Collegeville, MN: Liturgical Press, 1982.

Jamison, Christopher. *Finding Happiness: Monastic Steps for a Fulfilling Life*. Collegeville, MN: Liturgical Press, 2009.

Kardong, Terrence G. *Pillars of Community: Four Rules of Pre-Benedictine Monastic Life*. Collegeville, MN: Liturgical Press, 2010.

McQuiston, John II. *Always We Begin Again: The Benedictine Way of Living*. 15th anniv. rev. ed. New York: Morehouse Publishing, 2011.

Schauble, Marilyn, and Barbara Wojciak, eds. *A Reader's Version of the Rule of Saint Benedict in Inclusive Language*. Erie, PA: Benedictine Sisters of Erie, 1989.

Tomaine, Jane. *St. Benedict's Toolbox: The Nuts and Bolts of Everyday Benedictine Living*. 10th anniv. rev. ed. New York: Morehouse Publishing, 2015.

Selected Resources for the Divine Office

Sutera, Judith. *Work of God: Benedictine Prayer*. Collegeville, MN: Liturgical Press, 1997.

Tickle, Phyllis. *The Divine Hours: A Manual for Prayer*. 3 vols. New York: Doubleday, 2000.

www.missionstclare.com: An ecumenical website offering on an online experience of Morning and Evening Prayer.

www.universalis.com: Liturgical and devotional resources of the Roman Catholic Church.

Index to Benedict's Rule by Chapter ☐

The book you are holding in your hands presents selections from the sixth-century Rule of Benedict. I included the text for most of Benedict's chapters, whole or in part. The chapters I did not include contain content similar to that found in the covered chapters. For the chapters of Benedict's Rule used in this book, page numbers show you where you can find selections from each chapter of the Rule. Chapters not included follow this list.

Chapters in the Rule of Benedict Not Excerpted in this Book